CUSTOMER-CENTRIC

MARKETING

Keep it Simple
Keep it Human
Keep your Customer

Keep it Simple
Keep it Human
Keep your Customer

CUSTOMER-CENTRIC

MARKETING

Build Relationships, **Create** Advocates, and **Influence** Your Customers

ALDO
CUNDARI
CHAIRMAN & CEO,
CUNDARI GROUP LTD.

WILEY

For general information about our other products and services, please contact our Customer Care Department within the United States at (800) 762-2974, outside the United States at (317) 572-3993 or fax (317) 572-4002.

Wiley publishes in a variety of print and electronic formats and by print-on-demand. Some material included with standard print versions of this book may not be included in e-books or in print-on-demand. If this book refers to media such as a CD or DVD that is not included in the version you purchased, you may download this material at http://booksupport.wiley.com. For more information about Wiley products, visit www.wiley.com.

Library of Congress Cataloging-in-Publication Data:

Cundari, Aldo.
    Customer-centric marketing : build relationships, create advocates, and influence your customers/Aldo Cundari.
        pages cm
        Includes index.
        ISBN 978-1-119-09289-6 (cloth); ISBN 978-1-119-10261-8 (ePDF); ISBN 978-1-119-10265-6 (ePub)
        1. Relationship marketing.   2. Customer relations.   3. Marketing—Management.   I.   Title.
        HF5415.55.C86 2015
        658.8'12—dc23

                                                          2015002783

Printed in the United States of America

10 9 8 7 6 5 4 3 2 1

DEDICATED TO MY DARLING WIFE, LIVIAN, AND FIVE INCREDIBLE children, Natalie, Christopher, Julia, Joseph, and Nicholas, who mean the world to me. I further dedicate this book to my Mom and Dad for taking that leap of faith to fulfill their dreams for a better life and settling in Canada. My heart will always belong to you.

CONTENTS

PRELUDE

ALONG WITH THE OVERWORK AND HYPER-SPEED ENVIRONMENT that fills our day, the dedication and hard work involved in a project like this doesn't come along without the patience and support of some very talented individuals. It is their innovative spirit and creative talent for seeing what is just around the corner that makes our organization successful. So I thank all those who provided their input (thoughts and sweat) into making this book possible.

There are also people you meet in life who make a mark on you and, over time, they exit and reenter as though these encounters are destined and purposeful. Doug Moxon is one of those people. In the mid-1990s, Doug ran my U.S. regional office. After he left, we always stayed in touch, as if there were unfinished business. And this book is that unfinished business. Doug helped with the heavy lifting of research, editing, and being my debating partner for the ideas and concepts you will find in this book.

Let me also thank all those who have helped with their guidance and wisdom over the years and give a special shout-out to the many valued individuals who took the time to read the manuscript and provide their input. One in particular was Ronnie Cohen, who gave her time, energy, and love of writing to edit the book. I give my sincere thanks to the numerous employees, clients, and industry peers who have placed their trust in me and played important parts along this long journey. You make every day seem like it's a new beginning.

INTRODUCTION

The Shoemaker's Story

THE STARTING POINT FOR THIS BOOK CAME A COUPLE OF YEARS ago, when after a 30-year absence, I reengaged with my love of fine art and sculpture. As a young man I had studied fine arts and intended to pursue a career as a sculptor. Since it was the late 1970s, I went off to the local library (definitely pre-Internet) to look for a school in Italy to explore my creative aspirations. I discovered the Istituto Europeo di Disegno in Rome, Italy. So off I flew to Rome to apply, gain acceptance, and become a fine artist.

It wasn't quite what I expected. On the expected side, my studies exposed me to classical approaches to design and form, and enabled me, as a sculptor, to look at an object that has no form and see the form within it. I think that foresight has given me the ability to get to solutions more quickly. The unexpected was the practical side of creating fine art. You had to consider how the materials and installation affected the final viewer experience, so I studied industrial and architectural design, plus materials handling in order to work with the physical realities of the installation space. In hindsight, this combination of creative thinking and fact-based analysis established the basic framework for my future marketing mind-set.

INSPIRATION WHERE YOU'D LEAST EXPECT IT

While in Italy, I had a second and probably more profound experience that influenced my thinking. It took place on one of my school holiday breaks. My limited funds didn't allow me to fly back home to Canada, so I went to visit my parents' Italian birthplace in Rende, Calabria—a small village nestled in the hills of Cosenza, a southern Italian province. As I walked the streets of the small town, I could feel the rhythm of the community where my parents grew up and the life they left behind. Wandering through the central square, the Piazza Giuseppe Garibaldi, I overheard a conversation between a shoemaker and one of his loyal customers. This simple but personal conversation shaped my perspective on how to build long-lasting customer relationships, and I have illustrated it in the following story:

> *My grandfather lived in a small town of about 500 people in southern Italy. In the town was a shoemaker. He was a great shoemaker and learned the trade from his father and his father's father. He knew practically everyone in the town: how many kids they had, when he had made their last pair of shoes, and what kind of shoes they needed and liked. He could see them, talk to them, and check how fast their shoes were wearing out. He literally knew his market on a first-name basis. He could anticipate their needs and next purchase. If something went wrong, he could make it right, fast. He was always there with exactly what they wanted— when they wanted it.*
>
> **He provided an exceptional level of what we now call customer centricity and experience, and that's how he ensured his customers' loyalty.**

When I returned to North America and the realities of making a buck set in, I soon discovered opportunities for aspiring sculptors were very limited. It was time for Plan B, and I decided to use my creative skills to freelance at a few design and advertising firms. After I got some initial experience in the industry, I realized I had a unique advantage: I knew how to both frame a problem *and* create its solution. By employing my creative and analytic skills learned in Rome, I was able to turn around projects and solutions faster than my fellow creatives. In short order, this led to starting my own shop, which has since grown into a multidisciplined agency offering traditional and digital services to a broad range of global brands.

Only when I started to sculpt again did I realize that my business beliefs and practices were still heavily influenced by those early years in Rome. In particular, the study and discipline of classical art and the remarkable conversation between the shoemaker and his customer both played pivotal roles in the development of my business mind-set. These two experiences gave me a creative, analytic, and customer-centric lens on which to base my business approach/philosophy.

THE AGE OF THE CUSTOMER

In hindsight, I believe my formative time in Rome not only contributed to my past success but also will be even more important to me tomorrow. We all know the age of the customer is here to stay, and while its arrival has had a rather disruptive impact on the world economy, I believe it will continue to drive exponential change in the foreseeable future. Innovation and information are at the heart of this shift, and there is a lot of both. Enabled by a constant stream of new digital and social technologies, customers sit in the middle of an information tsunami. Their instant and convenient access to information has empowered their decision-making abilities, and their immediate access to community helps them confirm their choices and influence others. Pity the business that still uses only traditional marketing communications methods; it must be struggling to keep up with this pace, and its long-term prospects are dim.

Conversely, the current marketing ecosystem offers us many exciting opportunities. I'd like to share with you some of what I've learned in navigating these waters and how you can use this fundamental change in customer relationships to enhance your brand's marketing efforts and thrive in this new marketing environment.

This book is slightly different from the current crop of business books describing how to connect with customers in our transparent digital world. Don't get me wrong; there are many great books out there from renowned authors backed by first-rate research. But I'm more of a practitioner than a researcher, so you will find my observations and insights come from the realities of the street. With over three decades of hands-on, eyes-wide-open experience to tap into, I've accumulated lots of "lessons learned" and, with them, some ideas on how businesses, even individuals, can thrive in this new marketplace.

I certainly don't have all the answers. Sorry, I have yet to find the "silver bullet"; in fact, I still have lots of questions myself. That is what's so remarkable about this environment. If you're willing to get out there and take some risks, you'll find that today's digitally powered analytics systems will very quickly tell you how you're doing and will provide immediate and continual feedback, and with those answers will come even more questions.

My shoemaker tale started me thinking about how my insights and experience could help move brands forward in this new age. To face an enhanced level of customer centricity, we need a new marketing approach, a game plan, that encourages and rewards customer involvement. We may need to reconfigure our organizations, and we definitely need a new mind-set—one that is built on attracting, engaging, and retaining customers at every touchpoint, on and offline. This will be the new definition of success.

So that's what this book is about. Who are these new customers, why are they behaving so differently from the past, and how can we build long-lasting relationships that work for them and our business going forward?

Welcome to *Customer-Centric Marketing*. Please feel free to contact me at aldo_cundari@cundari.com or through any other social channel. I'd relish hearing your thoughts once you're done reading.

NOTE: CUSTOMER VERSUS CONSUMER

While often interchangeable, there is a small difference between the terms *customer* and *consumer*. Using *customer* implies you (or a competitor) already have established a relationship—she's no longer just a prospect for your product or service. *Consumer*, as used in the advertising and marketing world, implies someone who could use your (or a competitor's) product or service. Given these minor distinctions, let's use *customer*—I think it's more desirable.

CHAPTER ONE

THE AGE OF THE CUSTOMER

How Did We Get Here?

EVERY YEAR, AS PART OF STAYING IN TOUCH WITH OUR CLIENTS' customers, I visit retail locations to observe how customers behave in-store and how well the floor staff and sales associates are interacting with them throughout the sales process.

A couple of years ago, on a warm and sunny Saturday morning, I visited one of our automotive client's dealerships to spend a morning observing customers in order to get an idea of the car-buying experience from a customer's perspective. I watched for a while and then spent some one-on-one time with several of the sales associates to discuss how the sales process was working. On this day, the dealership was filled with customers shopping for new vehicles, always a welcome sight, but it was really *how* they were shopping that caught my attention—it felt completely different than just a few years back.

Customers were less interested in product information and more interested in taking a test drive, deciding on the spot, and negotiating an offer. This differed from just a few years ago, when the average customer would visit a dealership at least three times before beginning to negotiate a price. They needed these multiple visits to build up their product knowledge prior to making their final decision.

Today, the opposite holds true. Before visiting a dealership, customers have spent countless hours online researching brands. They've gathered information, read consumer reviews and influencer opinions, and used their social networks to get first-hand experiences from known third parties. They've probably also spent time on the brand's website, maybe building a car online with their desired, optional features, and perhaps they have even reviewed multiple financing options as well. They've done their homework. Armed with the information needed to make an informed decision, only then do they visit the dealership (whose customer reviews they've also checked out), arrange for a test drive, and negotiate a deal based on their pricing research.

Yes, these are the new car customers—sometimes more knowledgeable than the salesperson who waits on them! So that is our challenge: How do we influence these new customers, give them the information they need to make decisions, and anticipate their questions before they arrive at the dealership?

For our automotive client, we've tried a number of things such as making online content more interactive, linking to external reviews and blogs, monitoring social forums (including online communities) to see what people are talking about, and training product specialists and sales teams to be up to speed with current trends. Essentially, everyone on the sales floor needs to be confident, knowledgeable, and prepared to meet the needs of every customer who walks into the showroom. And while these seem to be working, we've only just scratched the surface—we know there'll be more changes to come.

SOLUTIONS COME THROUGH UNDERSTANDING

The dealership story is a micro-example of what is happening today. The last decade has witnessed a massive shift in how we market products and services. Driven by digital technologies, social media, hyper-competition, product proliferation, globalization, and changing customer behaviors, a new marketing era is upon us with a vengeance. And the most dramatic element of this new era is an empowered customer who is leveraging information through all things digital at a frenzied pace, making the world of marketing a much more challenging place for marketers. Just keeping up in this customer-driven, real-time environment requires a huge commitment.

The digitization of daily life has acted as a catalyst for the emergence of new customer behaviors, and as a result, has created fundamental changes in how business is done today. I've spent a lot of time in the trenches, not just in the auto market, but with other consumer and business-to-business (B2B) products and services, and with this field-tested experience, I have developed different strategic approaches on how to connect with this elusive, discerning customer. My hope is to reduce the confusion and shine a simple but powerful light on how to succeed in this new environment.

Over the last 10 years, I've invested a lot of time in understanding how these new and evolving customer behaviors influence our current business practices. I have channeled this learning into a strategic approach that has enabled my team and me to redesign and retool our organization to succeed in this new environment. As a result, we have built a business model that enables us to help our clients take advantage of new opportunities and win in this complex marketplace. In the following chapters, I'll share some of this learning and provide you with market-tested tools to evaluate your organization's readiness, including cultural and operating system changes that you may need to consider in order to prosper in this customer-centric marketing environment.

THE ROAD FROM GROUND ZERO

Before we dive in, lets establish some context on how we arrived at this major economic, cultural, and societal shift and set the stage for answering the big question:

"Where do we go next with this new, empowered customer?"

We'll start at ground zero of marketing to get an appreciation of where we've come from. As we look back through modern economic times, it's interesting to plot economic change against the evolution of marketing and see how these changes contribute to today's marketing environment. The way marketing change has played off economic change, and vice versa, demonstrates how innovations in both fields have moved us through a variety of marketing "eras" to our current situation (see Figure 1.1).

The *Industrial Revolution*[1] started the evolution to modern marketing by taking the world out of the simple barter system into a new age of manufactured goods. The first (1760–1840) and second (1840 to the 1920s) *Industrial Ages* created the last major shift in society. One of the most important outcomes was that average incomes experienced unprecedented and sustained growth, leading to the birth of the middle class. In the words of Nobel Prize winner Robert E. Lucas Jr., "For the first time in history, the living standards of the masses of ordinary people have begun to undergo sustained growth. . . . Nothing remotely like this economic behavior is mentioned by the classical economists, even as a theoretical possibility."[2] Driven by new manufacturing processes, the Industrial Revolution produced a wave of inventions and innovations that changed almost every aspect of daily life and marked a major turning point in history. Sound familiar?

THE AGE OF THE CUSTOMER ROAD MAP

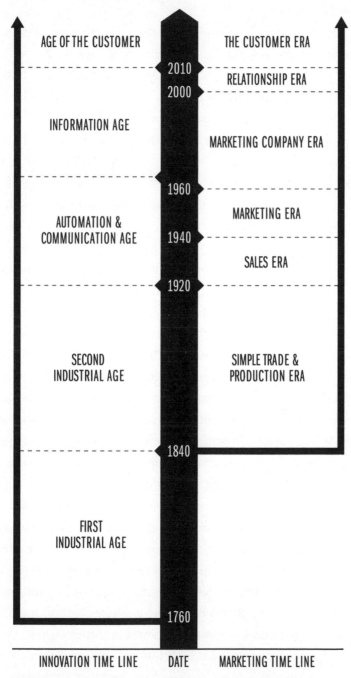

Figure 1.1   Innovation and marketing time line.[3]

Its impact on society parallels the incredible changes we are witnessing today.

The Industrial Ages spread innovative solutions and new manufacturing processes across different industries, and created a wide variety of goods in all sectors of the economy. Initially, because of low volumes, all goods were purchased. However, manufacturing efficiencies and outputs improved, and a middle class emerged wanting to buy these goods, spawning the *Automation and Communication Age* (1920–1965). During this period, production exceeded demand and competition became a marketplace reality. With competition firmly in place, businesses were forced to add employees to sell their goods. This period was known as the *Sales Era*.

The Automation and Communication Age continued until World War II intervened, and manufacturing resources were redirected to meet the needs of the war effort. It was North American manufacturers, primarily in the United States, that gave the Allies a decisive advantage in winning the war. At the conclusion of World War II, America emerged, unlike war-ravaged Europe, with a massive manufacturing base at its disposal, which had to be repurposed for peacetime and the pent-up demand for goods from a population who had sacrificed so much during the war years. This gave rise to mass marketing and the *Marketing Era*, which introduced early advertising and other marketing disciplines into the selling process. Technology evolved during this period, too, and set the stage for the *Information Age*. In particular, television's arrival added an exciting new dimension to the marketing mix.

As the 1960s moved forward, marketers capitalized on this new medium and were able to get their selling message to millions of viewers in 60 or even 30 seconds. Consumerism became a defining part of our lives, and marketing became an integral part of our culture. This age introduced the Marketing Era, which added more complexity to the marketing mix by moving beyond product marketing to disciplines such as customer research, segmentation, and branding.

The Automation and Communication Age was then followed by the Information Age (1965–2010), which is still a vital part of today's economic and marketing environment and the breeding ground for a wave of technological innovations that continue to change our world. Initially, information technologies contributed to the improvement of the manufacturing process. Efficiency and quality skyrocketed and allowed countries such as Japan, Korea, and China to become global players. We also ushered in a new age of distribution, as manufacturers were able to move products around the globe. From a marketing perspective, new information technologies (e.g., databases, increased processing speeds, powerful desktop computers) enabled the introduction of relational databases to build the framework for customer profiling and early database marketing. Evolving digital technologies increased the speed of innovation (it seems like we have an industrial revolution every couple of years now) and created a new economic order as the Web took off. This period brought high-speed bandwidth, social media, mobile phones, and other advances into the mix. During this age, marketing expanded its footprint and importance across all industries and built a broad range of sophisticated services and capabilities. This expansion was known as the *Marketing Company Era*.[4]

Still in the Information Age, the Marketing Company Era gave way to the *Relationship Era* approximately 10 years ago.[5] The Relationship Era capitalized on the same digital technologies that were powering the Marketing Company Era, but now there was exponential improvement and performance in the technologies at the marketers' disposal.[6] (Think of Moore's Law: Computing speed doubles every 18 months.)

The Relationship Era took the first steps toward customer centricity, but organizations still had a brand-first/customer-second pecking order. As the power of digital technologies enabled the customer to take the upper hand, the relationship started to flip. I call this current stage the *Age of the Customer*, and what an age it's turning out to be.

THE AGE OF THE CUSTOMER

I believe we moved from the Information Age to the Age of the Customer about 10 years ago, when the adoption of social media started to gain traction in the marketplace. Social media had been concentrated with early adopters, but the trend was clear. The introduction of smartphones pushed connectivity to new levels of performance and accessibility and added a new screen to the customer's portfolio of devices.

These early and hyper-speed adoption rates were indicators of things to come and the transition of power to the connected customer. The Information Age really got the digital world moving. Customers could go online, get pricing and inventory availability, and buy. In essence, it created a new sales channel for the marketing team. The Age of the Customer is much more disruptive and has dramatically changed how customers behave, purchase, and engage brands. There's no going back.

"Beware of not meeting customer needs, because if you don't, they'll just move on."

Since the Industrial Age, the pattern of innovation has been fairly consistent. Manufacturing and business innovations would stimulate new marketing practices, which would then be used to persuade customers to open their wallets and, hopefully, become loyal customers. In the last decade, the sequence has been reversed, and now the customer is dictating the terms of engagement. With this new leadership role, the customer has shaken up how marketing takes place. I call this the Age of the Customer from an economic perspective, and the *Customer Era* in the marketing time line.

In previous eras, innovations in manufacturing, information, and communications sparked new marketing practices. These practices were mainly driven by the marketer and unaffected by the hands of the customers, but in this new era, it's the customers who have a prominent and leading role in the relationship (see Figure 1.2), and we're even seeing their increased participation in strategic planning, product development, and marketing program development. While the Customer Era is still in its early stages, it is most obviously played out in the behavior of the young Gen Y or Millennial

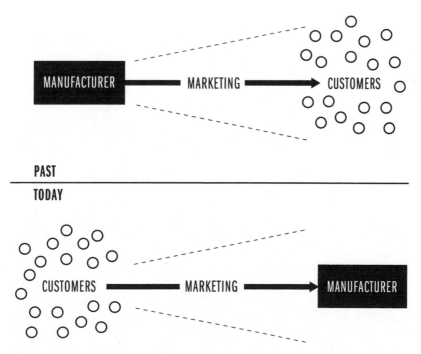

Figure 1.2   The new pecking order.

generation. This new customer–brand dialogue signals that a new pecking order is in play between customers and organizations, and if you are ignoring the shift, you are doing so at your own peril.

CHAPTER TWO

CARPE DIEM

The CMO Dilemma

FOR THE LAST 24 YEARS, I HAVE BEEN A MEMBER OF MAAW (Marketing Agencies Association Worldwide). This worldwide peer-to-peer group of independent marketing communications executives comes together twice yearly to share knowledge, ideas, and innovations. We also invite thought-provoking and trendsetting guest speakers from around the world to come join us.

I recently traveled to New York to attend a conference where one of our guest speakers was Paul Stoddart, head of advertising, strategic and competitive projects for Microsoft. Paul spoke about a new initiative he was leading there called Agile Marketing.

Agile Marketing takes a data-centric insight approach to fuel rapid development, experimentation, and optimization at the company. This same approach is also used as the basis for a new way of operating with their agencies.

It's built on a customer-responsive model for creative, production, and media that enables concept-to-market execution across all channels in as little as 14 days. It simply strips away all bureaucracy and focuses on being quick and agile in responding to data insights. It may sound incredible, but this small, flexible 15-person

Microsoft team, along with its small and agile agency, delivers full-channel campaigns in a matter of days, versus what used to take Microsoft months to achieve. This concept is best illustrated in the formula:

$$\text{Velocity} \times \text{Mass} = \text{Momentum}$$

Paul noted that Microsoft recognizes that small-sized agencies fit this formula best, as they too have an inherent velocity to their approach and less bureaucracy to their organization. That's why they have opted recently to work with smaller agencies—they both want momentum, and they will both fail if they get bogged down in "process."

The pace at which Paul's team operates provides a glimpse into the future of marketing, which is changing at a breakneck pace. There's no better place to see the impact of these marketing shifts than in the office of the chief marketing officer (CMO). It takes a brave CMO (or any executive) to face and deal with the complex factors redefining the marketing function. I use *brave* deliberately, because as the Microsoft initiative illustrates, it's a new world out there, and marketers can't rely on traditional marketing, advertising, and research practices to produce the same level of predictability and success they experienced in the recent past.

"Insanity: doing the same thing over and over again and expecting different results."

ALBERT EINSTEIN

On their own, traditional marketing solutions are proving to be a poor match for today's demanding customers. Marketers need to shake off previous beliefs and embrace a new way of thinking that thrives on being empathetic, innovative, analytical, adaptive, and connected.

THE EXTERNAL CHALLENGES YOU WILL FACE

So how has the brand–customer connection changed? Let's start with mass media. In terms of customer reach and efficiency, it once was a reliable channel. But its reduced efficiencies are due to new media choices, as well as an irrevocable change in customer behavior. Mass media's demise is fostered by the emergence of savvy customers who tune out brand messaging. In addition, these same customers have learned and benefited from a digital transparency that removes any barriers between your brand and them. The result? Suddenly, organizational secrets aren't so secret anymore, and insider revelations can be shared worldwide when someone hits Send. Somewhat less dramatically, traditional media's reduced influence is mirrored in the customer decision-making process. Customers now do their own research independent of the brand, use a variety of sources, and share that information with their community throughout the decision-making journey. Good or bad, there's nowhere to hide.

THE INTERNAL CHALLENGES YOU WILL FACE

Beyond product attributes, performance, and the purchasing process, business values have also become a determining factor in a customer's brand preferences. In the Marketing Company and Relationship Eras, customers were relatively content with the goods and services offered. In those times, the relationship was based on a simple promise by the brand to deliver value, and the customer trusted the brand to deliver on its promise. Now, a company's values need to sync with customers' values and beliefs and must deliver on their shared values. *For the customer, it increasingly comes down to trust.*

If a company doesn't live up to its promise and values, it doesn't take long before everyone knows it. Transparency has taken the brand–customer relationship to a new level. Trust has expanded to include how companies act in the world, and if the trust is broken, at any level, customers will walk. And not only will they walk— they will tell others about it, too.

THE MULTIPLIER EFFECT

Customers tell others about their customer service experiences, both good and bad.[1] Customers say they tell an average of 9 people about good experiences, and nearly twice as many (16 people) about poor ones. On the other hand, 7 in 10 customers (70 percent) are willing to spend an average of 13 percent more with companies they believe provide excellent customer service (see Figure 2.1).

GOOD EXPERIENCES

POOR EXPERIENCES

CUSTOMERS TELL NEARLY TWICE AS MANY PEOPLE
(16 ON AVERAGE) ABOUT POOR EXPERIENCES

Figure 2.1   The Multiplier Effect.

With so many opportunities for customers to interact with your brand, it becomes increasingly difficult to make sure all your bases are covered. But there are ways of moving forward and working through these challenges. As I mentioned, we need to start by pushing old conventions of thinking aside, adopting a new set of rules, and embracing the needs of the newly empowered customer. At its heart, this refocused marketing mind-set starts with the voice of the customer, and this voice will be the catalyst for your brand's and business's growth. In most cases, your brand will be tested on the front lines, so it's critical that all customer-facing employees understand and represent the brand's values at every stage of the purchase decision journey.

Success in this new Customer Age rides on the shoulders of the CMO and the marketing team, who are best positioned to tackle the challenge of being the customer's champion. Their formidable task starts with seeding and enforcing (through training and recruiting) a customer-centric approach throughout the organization to ensure the customer experience is represented clearly and consistently at every touchpoint.

"Success in this new Customer Era rides on the shoulders of the CMO and the marketing team, who are best positioned to be the champion of the customer."
Think of it as a marketing renaissance.

With those challenges in mind, how prepared are CMOs? A recent global CMO study found CMOs across all regions were struggling to keep up with the seismic changes shaking their organizations.² Five challenges registered the highest levels of unpreparedness:

- 71 percent of CMOs rated the data explosion as their number one concern. As we now create as much data in two days as we did from the dawn of civilization to 2003, it's not surprising that CMOs are challenged by the velocity and variety of data coming at them from all directions.

- 68 percent see social media as an immense challenge, as it is dramatically different from traditional media and establishes a layer of transparency that is anything but comfortable.

- 65 percent rate growth of channel and device choices as a concern and struggle to manage the "all you can eat buffet" of devices and channels with limited organizational resources and expertise.

- 63 percent feel shifting customer demographics will dramatically impact their marketing functions, but only 37 percent are prepared for the different needs, consumption habits, and communications preferences that come with the new customer and generational behavior shifts.

- Over 63 percent say return on involvement (ROI) will be the most critical indicator of success over the next three to five years, but only 44 percent feel prepared to manage the increasing importance of ROI.

IGNORE THE VOICE OF DOOM; IT'S ONLY A VOICE

You can look at the mission of CMOs from two perspectives: One, they're doomed; two, what a great opportunity! More than anything, a lack of vision and preparedness for what's coming can impact an organization's ability to effectively deal with and engage today's customer. Traditional sources of information that once drove strategic decisions don't quite work in an on-demand, real-time marketing world.

In our quickly evolving business environment, new and continually refreshed sources of information are required. If you base future planning on traditional analytics, you're getting old insights and data that significantly lag behind what's really going on or about to happen. You're not seeing current customer behavior or transactional trends in real time, and you're left to operate from a position of weakness, not strength, when it comes to producing positive customer experiences and a healthy bottom line. It's no wonder that traditional marketing is having a hard time keeping customers interested.

Even as organizations struggle to keep up, customers are engaging brands on their own terms and building perceptions derived from trusted sources such as friends, family, and influencers. Not surprisingly, traditional marketing-communication approaches have a hard time competing and captivating in this environment. As we compete with these new factors, brands must become customer-centric and provide value at every stage of the customer purchase journey, from initial awareness through postpurchase.

To effectively measure customer experience and take advantage of the findings, you need real-time connections, not metrics that are long gone. The Shoemaker Story I described in the Introduction is a real-world example of what companies should strive for today. The shoemaker's frequent and personal customer interaction provided him with data that translated into insights he could use to quickly identify, preempt, or resolve issues. His use of customer knowledge to provide better customer experiences delivers a valuable lesson for today's marketer.

BREAKING DOWN THE TRADITIONAL MIND-SET

At the root of many organizational bottlenecks is a traditional mind-set. This dated perspective holds back key customer experience initiatives. It's not too surprising, because in the not-too-distant past, operations and IT drove organizational change through the pursuit of greater efficiencies and profitability in areas such as manufacturing processes or high-speed networks. From a business capabilities perspective, these remain important assets, but it's now time for customer centricity to take the lead in the organization's quest for success.

This is no easy task for CMOs—these organizational bottlenecks are difficult to overcome. They need to have steadfast beliefs in their convictions and a commitment to fight for the operating capabilities, technologies, and talent required to deliver an optimal customer experience. And while they're doing that, they need to make smaller budgets work harder and implement programs that consistently deliver a positive ROI. And lastly, as the organization's customer champion, the CMO must ensure that customer touchpoints across the organization align under one direction and experience.

"Touchpoints can't be managed as isolated silos with separate programs; otherwise, the strength of the customer–brand relationship becomes a weakness."

NO BETTER TIME TO GET STARTED THAN NOW

CMOs and their teams can start by monitoring every customer touchpoint, collecting data, and sharing learning. Access online communities, forums, review sites, and social media such as Facebook and Twitter, and connect directly with customers. Spend a day in their shoes. Commit your organization to getting up close and personal when collecting customer information, and you will develop the empathy and capacity to improve their experience.

By acting now, instead of waiting to see what "new technology" happens down the line, you gain some definite and significant competitive advantages. For example, there are surprisingly inexpensive and easy-to-use social media monitoring tools available right now that can work to your advantage. Some of these quick fixes provide key insights on customer sentiment, usage, and preferences, and those insights provide a golden opportunity to build a deeper understanding of customer behavior and needs.

To enable CMOs, new digital platforms and media can be used to support a customer-centric strategy. Tools currently at their disposal include social media listening platforms, real-time big data analytics, sophisticated customer-needs segmentation, and personalization applications. There are multiscreen environments that offer a myriad of ways to connect with customers—more than ever before. However, while there are lots of digital options, you don't need to use them all. Make your selection based on the needs and habits of your customers. And don't neglect to take advantage of your employees' knowledge; you have Millennials on staff that can be in-house reference points for what's going on in their world.

Many organizations are poorly equipped to grow their business in this customer-centric age because they still operate in an old paradigm. That means a forward-looking marketing team has a unique advantage. By using new business tools to support and measure customer experience, the marketing team can enhance and build relationships with its customers, while providing valuable leadership within its organization.

Potentially, the most challenging job is evangelizing the importance of the customer-centric business model to the C-suite and ensure its buy-in to this new way of doing business. CMOs have a lot resting on their shoulders, but with their customer expertise—

which affects every aspect of a business' operations—they also have the credibility and knowledge to bring divergent operating units together to focus on the customer.

To grow and strengthen customer relationships, you must make their experience valuable and consistent at every level of contact. A CMO's ability to fulfill such a challenging mandate is hampered by technology and sociocultural advances that are often evolving faster than we can adapt. For example, in 2013 I participated in a CMO research study conducted by the Institute of Communication Agencies (ICA). The study's goal was to learn more about the changing dynamics of the marketing function in Canada. Study participants were CMOs and senior-level marketing executives from a variety of brands across the marketing spectrum.[3] During a day-long session, we discussed the challenges, opportunities, and rewards that characterize today's marketing environment.

As you can imagine, it was a lively discussion, and here are some of my salient takeaways:

- An ever-increasing focus on ROI means there is little time to think and no time to fail. It is increasingly difficult to reconcile fast decisions and results to meet a quarterly focus with long-term strategic planning, which in turn makes it easy to compromise work. Consistency can also take a hit, as the need for short-term results encourages you to take actions that might not work over the longer term.

- With information overload, it's easy to feel lost. Data can be plentiful and easy to access, but instead of helping, it often complicates decision making and analysis.

- The new power of customers is exciting but challenging. With their newfound power, customers can be incredible brand ambassadors for brands they like or brand assassins for those they don't. They want to be part of the conversation, but only on subjects that interest and engage them. Building a good customer experience by properly matching content in the correct traditional, digital, or social media channels with the customers' position in their purchase journey is very challenging. It's even harder to ensure all customer-facing employees are working off the same page when it comes to delivering a consistent customer experience across all interaction points.

- The pace of change has resulted in steep learning curves. The combination of new global players, exponential growth of digital technologies and channels, fragmentation of traditional and new media, and shifting customer behavior together have forced CMOs to be in a constant state of knowledge acquisition. Change is definitely the only constant, and having enough time to stay abreast of new developments is problematic.

- An increased need for specialized expertise makes some marketers feel they need to be "general contractors" on top of their other responsibilities. With so many new things to learn and disciplines within disciplines, the traditional agency relationship doesn't cover all the bases. As a consequence, agencies are no longer considered one-stop shops, and loyalty is not a given. Conversely, when marketers have to deal with a lot of different suppliers, they then must navigate through a myriad of unique business practices, such as financial management, which adds another layer of complexity to their responsibilities.

- An ongoing challenge is setting and keeping everyone in the organization committed to providing a consistent customer experience. There are multiple employees connecting with customers, and they each need to provide an experience that reflects the values of the brand, regardless of customer touchpoint or context.

- It takes a lot of courage to be a marketer, and it can be dangerous! As marketing needs evolve around the CMO's team, marketers have to get in the game even if their understanding is incomplete. Time is in short supply these days, and CMOs need to be confident and comfortable combining facts with intuition to get programs out the door.

These findings reemphasize that today's CMOs have to keep a lot of balls in the air as they try to keep pace or reinvent their marketing process. One of the biggest challenges is demonstrating to the organization that what they're doing is working. To make that happen, CMOs need to generate proof points that quantitatively prove they're on the right track. I recommend you start small and look for opportunities where you can create an immediate impact. By starting small, you can build your business gradually, which not only reduces your risk but also helps gain support from key stakeholders for your future initiatives.

THE CUSTOMER-CENTRIC CHECKLIST

With the business world moving toward customer centricity, how do you rate your organization? Here's a checklist to help you gauge your company's effectiveness in being a customer-centric organization. Once you complete this quiz (it should take 15 minutes or so) the rest of *Customer-Centric Marketing* will help you fill in any additional gaps that you discover.

CUSTOMER CENTRICITY (5 being High or YES and 1 being Low or NO)   1-5

CULTURE

Does your organization have someone focused on understanding the customer and ensuring everyone from the C-suite to no-suite understands the needs of the customer? (E.g., chief customer officer, customer evangelist, Advocate, etc.)

Are you, or your team, responsible for all internal and external customer touchpoints?

Does your organization have programs that support the postpurchase customer experience and other actions that encourage loyalty, community interaction, and repeat purchase?

Does your organization have someone responsible for coordinating all user experiences across all touchpoints?

Does your organization collect data to help shape engagement and experience strategies that match customer needs and exceed customer expectations?

ORGANIZATION

Is your organization structured traditionally in departmental silos?

Do senior executives regularly interact with employees on an informal and formal basis?

Does your organization empower employees to take responsibility for delivering on customer needs at every touchpoint?

Does your organization encourage team members to contribute and support ideas, strategies, and proposals?

MARKETING MANAGEMENT

Are you the brand champion in your organization and the gatekeeper for the brand's core values? If so, are these unifying forces across the business?

Does your office serve as the hub for customer and competitive intelligence?

Does your office provide real-time access to customer behavior/transactional intelligence for the entire organization?

Are you responsible for your organization's marketing strategy and its implementation?

Does your role and responsibility include unifying, motivating, mobilizing, and focusing marketing assets and partners to create the greatest market impact?

Does your role and responsibility include connecting and creating dialogue with product, sales, channel, line of business (LOB), and ops + finance teams, as well as inviting field input from both channel and internal/external sales groups?

RESEARCH	1-5
Are you or your team responsible for assigning and keeping the results of customer research?	
Do you and your team visit the marketplace regularly to observe, share, and document the customer purchase journey experience?	
Are you responsible for the development and distribution of customer insights to your organization?	
Are you responsible for the collection and analysis of customer and transactional data for your organization?	
Does your organization have someone responsible for marketing analytics and their relationship to key performance indicators (KPI) and traditional business-performance metrics?	
TOTAL	

Once you have taken the test, compare your organization to other organizations that have taken the same test. If you scored less than average, then you need to get busy creating and implementing the appropriate strategies to become a customer-centric organization.

86-90 You are a well-oiled customer-centric organization. Bravo!

80-85 You have a really solid customer-centric orientation, with some additional upside potential.

70-79 You are trying to get there, but you still have some work left.

60-69 You're doing okay, but you're on the cusp of being left behind.

50-59 You're not keeping up with the competition; it's make-or-break time.

< 50 We don't want to talk about it.

BUILDING A CUSTOMER-CENTRIC ORGANIZATION

Now that you know where your organization is in terms of its quest for customer centricity, you also can see what's required to take it to the next level. To get there quickly, you can jump to Chapter 7, which is filled with practical ideas to move your organization to a more customer-centric stance. Or stay with me a while longer as we take a walk down memory lane.

CHAPTER THREE

CUSTOMER RELATIONSHIPS HAVE CHANGED

---

*The Decline of Brand Trust and
Rise of the Brand Advocate*

WHILE WE EXPECT SO MUCH FROM THE CUSTOMER, THE customer is expecting even more back from the brand. And with history as our witness, customers (for the most part) are having trouble trusting brands, which means trouble for many businesses. Without a relationship based on trust, we are not likely to breed brand Advocates or even loyal customers who support us. Let's put the issue of brand trust in context.

We have all heard of David versus Goliath, and their mythical battle re-created for today when one individual armed with the power of social media takes on a corporate giant and wins. Well, it's no myth; it's now a business reality that happens daily in one form or another.

One example that has come to be known as the *United Breaks Guitars* video specifically comes to mind. This simple but effective message really set the benchmark for others to follow. The last time I viewed it on YouTube, the viewer count was at 14,347,854 (and I watched it twice more)—that's a lot of people who watched the video and shared the experience. To recap the story quickly, a battle started when United Airlines passenger Dave Carroll saw his beloved Taylor guitar get badly damaged on the tarmac by one of the airline's baggage handlers. After many attempts to get restitution from United failed, David did what he does best (music!) and wrote a very humorous song pointing out United Airlines' brutal customer service, which quickly became famous.

And it has stayed famous. Incidents like this tend to fade away in the social space, but not in the case of *United Breaks Guitars*—it just keeps getting bigger. The first month saw over 4 million viewers, which is a very significant viewership; however, since then there have been nearly 10 million additional views, as well as 25,864 comments (see Figure 3.1).[1]

Can you imagine if something like that happened to you—the impact on your brand? This demonstrates the power of the new customers and how they can endorse *or shame* your brand with lasting repercussions. In United's case, these repercussions included considerable damage to their stock value; one source estimated

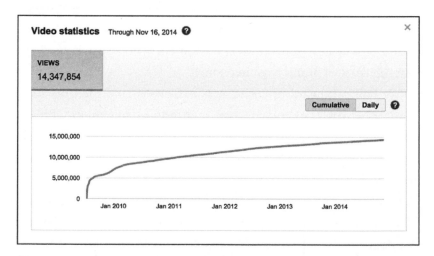

Figure 3.1   Total views of *United Breaks Guitars*.

that United lost 10 percent of their market cap, which might be a little over the top, but even if it was 1 percent of their market cap, that would be 1 percent too much.

Turn the clock back, and imagine if United had turned that dissatisfied customer into an Advocate instead—what positive power this incident would have delivered to its franchise. For example, if United had immediately and positively responded to Dave's request, maybe the singer-songwriter would have produced a second video to sing "United Saves the Day"—showing his guitar coming back to life. Unfortunately, United didn't have the technology or team in place then to address this in real time—so Dave took his problem to social media. Even worse, United chose to ignore Dave and in doing so turned an opportunity to demonstrate high corporate values and trustworthiness into a PR and financial nightmare. If only United had had a real-time marketing (RTM) response team listening for customer-centric opportunities and responding to them in real time.

As the story demonstrates, traditional marketers using traditional tactics make it nearly impossible to reach and respond quickly to today's customers. Opinionated, demanding, and supported by easy access to information through digital technologies, social media, and other online resources, these customers are forcing marketers and advertisers to play "catch me if you can." And while brands struggle to connect, customers are building a new set of relationships outside the brand's domain and sharing stories and opinions with on- and offline communities. To get brands back into the conversation, marketers need to change their approach and meet the requirements of the new brand–customer relationship.

CUSTOMERS ARE NOT CONNECTING THE WAY THEY USED TO

To understand how the marketing communications landscape has changed, let's start by looking at traditional media's reduced influence. For many years, network television was the go-to medium. Networks had a huge, dedicated viewership and created massive efficiencies in cost and reach for advertisers. To demonstrate this, let's go back to April 9, 1979. On that evening, the iconic *All in the Family* TV sitcom drew over 40 million viewers from a U.S. population that was almost a third smaller than what it is today.[2] Flash forward to April 9, 2012, and the final hour of prime time. The top five networks combined drew an audience of 29.7 million viewers. If you think those viewership numbers are mind-boggling, factor in that they include viewers with DVRs. One estimate puts DVR ownership levels at 40 percent of U.S. households, and among DVR owners, over 50 percent use them to skip commercials. Personally, I think the skip rate is higher.

If you're an advertiser wanting to block-book the same time on all five networks, you're probably reaching about 20 million viewers. That's providing they're not using the break to channel-surf, hit the kitchen, check e-mails, or chat with other viewers online who are watching the same show. Viewing options today are quite different from the limited channel selections of 1979, and customers can now choose from over hundreds of cable stations, TV on demand, or Web-based programming providers such as Hulu, YouTube, or Netflix. The good news is that segmented specialty channels help focus the message to the right target customers; the bad news is that with all the distractions from other information sources, getting their full attention is almost impossible. Not only that; if you're using a "mass market" or traditional media-planning model, you're doomed to death by fragmentation. So much viewing, so little time, and commercials are the first to be ignored.

Network TV is not the only medium feeling the pain. Publishing, another important element in the traditional marketing mix, is also under siege. In 1979, daily newspaper circulation in the United States was 62.2 million, but by 2011 it had dropped to 44.4 million, and ad revenue had plummeted by two-thirds. A main factor was the exodus of classified advertising to free websites like Craigslist or Kijiji. Magazines have done as poorly, and their ad revenues have dropped 42 percent since 2000. Many have tried reformatting (weeklies into biweeklies), but others have simply gone away: *Newsweek, Gourmet, Metropolitan Home, Teen, PC World*—that list goes on and on.

Traditional media's dramatically reduced influence demonstrates how essential it is for brands to realign their strategy and build programs that not only recognize new customer behaviors but also leverage the new digital media channels to create multiple engagement pathways. In the "not all gloom and doom category," look how AMC (among others) combines exceptional content, multiscreen access, online viewer communities, and even games to create winning television series such as *Breaking Bad* and *The Walking Dead*.

CUSTOMERS DON'T BELIEVE WHAT BRANDS SAY ANYMORE

As traditional brand-building media channels collapse or see their significance dramatically reduced, there is yet another barrier impacting brands' ability to connect with customers: trust.

Customer trust in brands has dropped precipitously—to almost unheard-of low levels. Looking at the 2008–2012 time period, dramatic declines in brand trust have taken place across the board. As Figure 3.2 demonstrates, smaller local businesses saw their brand trust scores go from 63 to 55 percent; large, national businesses' brand trust ratings went from 30 to 23 percent; and investment companies experienced a 26 to 18 percent drop in brand trust.

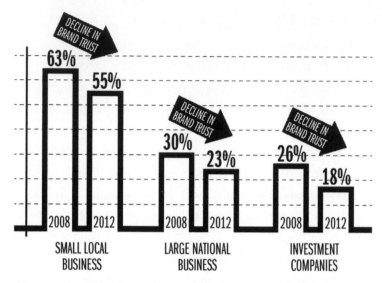

Figure 3.2   Decline in brand trust.[3]

This decline in trust vividly symbolizes the disconnect between what a brand says it is and what it actually does. More importantly, corrupt or disingenuous organizations can't hide anymore. With a smartphone in every pocket and social media at their disposal, customers are forcing transparency on businesses and governments whether they like it or not. As a consequence, a skeptical and independent perspective on brands and their promises has developed. Customers are looking elsewhere for credibility and rely on friends and third parties to decide whether a brand is trustworthy or not. To demonstrate, a 2013 study found that 70 percent of U.S. online adults trusted product recommendations from family and friends, followed by customer-written reviews at 46 percent. Only 10 percent trusted brand ads on websites, while only 9 percent trusted text messages from companies or brands.[4] The message is clear: If you think the media landscape is hard to navigate, gaining the trust of your customer is infinitely more challenging.

REBUILDING CONFIDENCE IN YOUR BRAND

How much influence do you really have? That is literally the million-dollar question, and businesses make a mistake when they apply traditional thinking to the Age of the Customer and its new customer-centric dynamic. It's no longer a funnel from awareness to purchase; this is a long, winding road, and you have to be there at the right time with the right message at every step of the way. One bad move (as the United Airlines story demonstrates) can reduce purchase intent and negate all the brand equity you have worked so hard to build over the years. To avoid negative outcomes, you need to empathize with your customers, make their needs your number one priority, and support them at every stage of their journey. If you are not delivering consistent, positive experiences, your customer is not going to connect with your brand at any touchpoint.

There is a glimmer of hope on the horizon, and it's the marketing team—it can be the hero. Marketing is uniquely positioned to play a leadership role in solving customer touchpoint issues. With its deep customer knowledge and strategic insights, marketing can and should guide the organization's customer-centric activities. Who is better prepared with the required focus, commitment, and understanding of customers' needs and wants required at every point of brand interaction and experience? To do this, you must be the keeper of your customers' total experience and make your customer the center of your business strategy.

So, in essence, developing customer trust is up to you. Success depends on your ability to put your best foot forward—to coordinate, adapt, and work within the constraints of the new customer-centric marketing ecosystem. And for those brave marketers who accept the challenge, that's the kind of initiative you and your organization should thrive on. You're going to have a brand that customers trust.

THE RISE OF THE BRAND ADVOCATE

You've been hearing a lot about how customers have fundamentally changed their purchasing behavior. As a marketer, you know they're traveling down a new road but aren't quite sure which map they're using. Customer focus or centricity may adorn many a mission or vision statement, but actually delivering on that promise is a totally different matter. Previously, customer-centric brands focused on extracting data about purchase behavior, creating insights, and channeling that into transactional programs and, hopefully, some brand loyalty. In practice, *customer centricity was created by pushing a brand-focused message onto segments of targeted customers.*

Today, customer centricity has a totally new meaning. Brands do not lead the relationship anymore. Instead, customers have taken over the driver's seat and are engaging with brands on their own terms. The level of engagement they choose is based on knowledge, perceptions, and experiences gathered from influencers in the on- and offline communities. That's where the customer starts to build a relationship with the brand. Then it's up to the brand to show up and meet their expectations in every nuance of the relationship— from product performance to postpurchase support to brand values. It's a long list, and every aspect of the brand is scrutinized and evaluated.

HOW ELSE HAVE CUSTOMERS BEEN TRANSFORMED?

Over the last decade, and particularly in the last five years, as smartphones and tablets have emerged as digital enablers, customers have evolved significantly. They have become hyper-connected, discriminating, and hard to win over. Their reluctance to engageis driven by the fact that they're bombarded by up to 5,000 messages a day and as a result, their precious time is overwhelmed with irrelevant information (see Figure 3.3). As James Gleick says in *Faster:*

"When information is cheap, attention becomes expensive."

Multiple digital devices with easy access, and lots of information, have transformed a traditionally linear buying process into a nonlinear experience with lots of constantly shifting parts. Mitch Joel in *Control Alt Delete* describes today's customers as "squiggly." Continually in motion, and with digital connections to influencers from around the globe, they're incredibly well informed

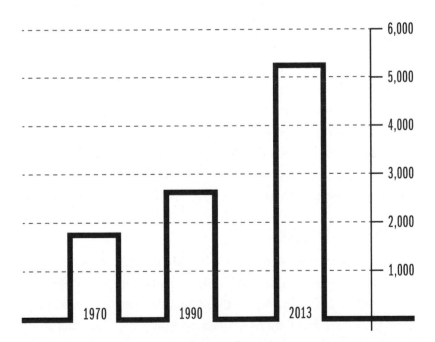

Figure 3.3   Average marketing messages per day (U.S. consumer).[5]

As a quick exercise, multiply the total numbers of messages per day by 365 days and then consider the amount of actual information customers receive—is it even possible to know what to trust with all that information? Customers having the means and opting to source information from people they trust starts to make a great deal of sense.

and accessing at every touchpoint with multiple digital devices. For brands, it's challenging to be part of the conversation, because, as we have established, customers don't have a high level of trust in what the brand has to say. So, when the brand does connect, the message can't disappoint—a bad experience will likely be shared with their connections and all their connections' connections.

As a result, *marketing has taken over the sales function* because of the way purchasing behavior has changed. Only marketing can connect with the customer in the early stages of the purchase journey, stay engaged until the final purchase decision, and then beyond to cultivate loyalty. Not to diminish the importance of your sales department, but if the customer is the queen bee, marketing is its drone.

THE RISE OF THE MILLENNIAL

Because of their digital savvy and culture, Millennials, our digital natives, are leading the customer transformation. Now between the ages of 18 and 34, they're going to be your customers for a long time. So, understanding what makes them tick and how your business matches their needs is incredibly important, because if you're not getting the job done now, in 10 years, when the Millennials start reaching middle age, you're probably not going to be around.

MILLENNIALS AREN'T ALONE

Make no mistake; as early adopters, Millennials are leading the profound changes in the way business is conducted. They have channeled digital technologies into valuable tools for making purchase decisions. But they're not alone—they have company in the form of a broader group called Generation C, where C stands for "connected." Gen C draws members from all age groups, and they are united by their decision to make all things digital an important part of their lifestyle.

According to Forrester Research, Gen C composition is predominantly made up of Millennials, but the Gen C mind-set is spreading as digital technologies make inroads into late adopters. Even with baby boomers, chances are that computers and the Web have been part of their workspaces and lives for years. Technology is not an unfamiliar part of their lives; it's just that baby boomers, and Gen X for that matter, didn't have access to all the cool stuff that's out there now. As they continue to see how technology makes life easier, more interesting, and perhaps even more valuable, it won't be long before even late adopters get on board.

BEHAVIOR ACROSS ALL AGES IS BEING TRANSFORMED

These behavioral shifts are occurring because getting connected, both physically and financially, has never been easier. Innovative digital technologies, combined with big bandwidth availability, has opened the connectivity floodgates to anyone who wants in. North American smartphone sales have now surpassed 140 million customers and are gaining strong penetration into the "late majority" of customers.[6] At the same time, tablet sales have surpassed 50 million (while PCs have lost significant market share)! Marketers are now dealing with customers who use a variety of digital screens and are always connected. When you consider the iPhone was launched in 2007, and the iPad in 2010, this transition has happened incredibly fast, and remarkably high adoption levels of digital technologies have created fundamental changes in how business and marketing are conducted. To illustrate, here's a snapshot of U.S. market trends:[7]

- From 2008 to 2012, PC usage dropped from 78 percent to 57 percent as mobile devices took a prominent place in the lives of customers.
- Smartphones are now owned by 60 percent of households, and tablets have been purchased by 30 percent of households with Internet access.

- Phones and tablets now use up 44 percent of personal computing time, almost doubling since 2008.
- Communication modes have shifted from voice to data and video. E-mail and telephonic voice have fallen from 80 percent to 60 percent of our "communications" portfolio; cell phones are now used for talking 20 percent of the time, with more time used for streaming music, browsing websites, and playing games.
- Social media usage has doubled, using 25 percent of communications time.
- Almost 50 percent of video viewing is on-time or device-shifted to laptops, tablets, or mobile phones.
- Over 60 percent of music usage comes from streaming devices, MP3 files, or satellite radio, leaving AM/FM radio with just a 32 percent share.
- Even among customers aged 55–64, mobile phone usage exceeds that of landlines.

Overall, these are startling trends, especially when you consider most of these shifts have happened in the last five years. With digital access available anytime, anywhere, marketers face the incremental challenge of producing content that works seamlessly across all platforms and matches the needs of customers during the different stages of their purchase journey. Good content is gold, and if you're simply repurposing content without considering the unique usage inherent in each digital device, you're wasting time and money, and hurting your business. So, it's time to reframe your marketing model and start connecting with customers before they move to greener pastures.

THE RISE OF THE BRAND ADVOCATE

One of the most important outcomes of this digital transformation is the rise of a new and very powerful customer—the Advocate.

Once known as Evangelists, these customers have dramatically increased their importance to your brand. With a globe gone digital and the power of social media, they have a platform to make their point of view known to everyone. Advocates have become incredibly valuable assets. Representing 16 to 20 percent of your customer base, they are brand believers and supporters, and in that role, influence the remaining 80 to 84 percent of your customers. Advocates are customers who write about your brand and share it with their personal, social, and business networks. You obviously need them on your side, because they have a disproportionate impact on persuading others to engage with and believe in your brand.

Getting the word out through customer endorsements is a prerequisite for brand success today. According to Everett Rogers's *Diffusion of Innovation Adoption Curve*, each category of adopters acts as an influencer and reference group for the next group. Rogers's theory was expanded by Chris Maloney to the "*Maloney 16 Percent Rule.*" He states that once you reach a 16 percent adoption rate for any innovation, it's time to change your messaging strategy from one based on scarcity to one based on social proof, in order to accelerate over the chasm and reach the masses. In this scenario, Advocates play a critical role in moving brands into new customer territories.

When I apply this thinking to a customer-centric context, it reminds me of how throwing a stone into a pond creates ripples that move outward in ever-increasing circles from the center to the pond's edge. Exchange the stone for an Advocate's positive post or recommendation, and you get an idea of how digital word of mouth works in today's connected world, and how Advocates' messaging accelerates your brand across the chasm (see Figure 3.4).

These Advocates are your evangelists and sharecasters, and when given the right content, they will reshape it and spread it—it becomes a permanent repository of comments from your most

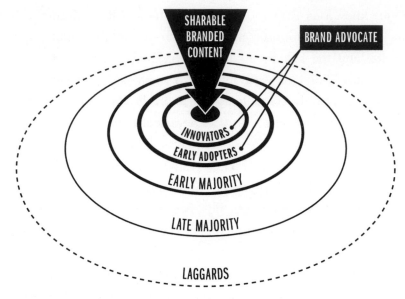

Figure 3.4   How Advocates spread their message.

valuable customers. Advocates are the early adopters of your product and will provide clear and concise feedback on the product. They will also be staunch defenders of your brand when it is attacked.

Because today's customers behave quite differently from those in the past, winning them and persuading them to become Advocates can be difficult. Customers have changed from being *passive* to being *active and engaged*, and Advocates exist on a level above that. It takes time and a disciplined series of interactions to build the right conditions for customer engagement, let alone advocacy, and it's never a conventional product message.

Increasingly, your organizational values and vision play an integral part in creating a relationship. Advocates, more than other customers, are examining and testing them regularly to make sure they continue to resonate with their own beliefs before they make a decision. That's the starting point, and the relationship will

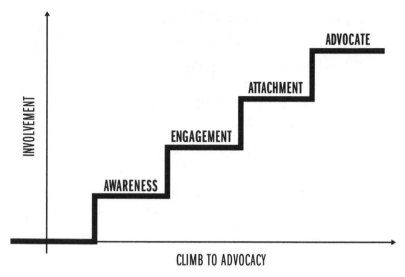

Figure 3.5   Becoming an Advocate.

change and evolve as you move through awareness, engagement, and attachment to Advocate stages of the customer relationship process. Only when they have bought, tried, and had a positive experience with your offering will they consider becoming an Advocate for your brand (see Figure 3.5).

1. *Awareness:* The starting point is always awareness. What do customers know about the brand and what the brand stands for? What are they saying to each other? Do they visit your website? How many page views? What is the visit duration? What do customer interest levels suggest?

2. *Engagement:* Beyond awareness, are customers interacting with you, clicking through ads, signing up for experiential events, registering with contact information, following social media feeds, and so on?

3. *Attachment:* Have customers strengthened their relationship and interacted with the brand by posting, blogging, and commenting/responding about the brand?

4. *Advocate:* The last stage is when they become Brand Advocates and are actively recommending you to friends, sending links, posting on social media, or participating in the brand user community.

PRIMING THE ADVOCATE PUMP

Customers move through the awareness, engagement, attachment, and Advocate stages when they have bought, tried, and had positive experiences with your offering. To convert them into Advocates, you need to start a different kind of conversation. Mark Twain provided a good insight into what it's going to take:

"You can make more friends in two months by being interested in other people than in two years by making people interested in you."

To start, you have to empathize with your prospective customers, understand their needs, and know how your product or service will make their lives better. From there, you need flawless product and service experiences, helpful and entertaining content, and access to insider knowledge. This combination encourages customers to turn into Advocates, and Advocates to persuade others in their social networks to join them: for example, "Here's a great video" or "Here's a special event you should check out." Not only are you providing value to Advocates, but also you're developing content for them to pass along to their social universe.

BMW 1M CASE STUDY

To demonstrate how a customer-centric focus can engage and excite Advocates, here's a great example from the 2012 launch of the BMW 1 Series M Coupé. BMW had spent many years promoting the *Joy of Driving*, but with the launch of the BMW 1 Series M Coupé, there was an opportunity to communicate the brand's high-performance credentials. By engaging the brand's Advocates with great content in multiple, entertaining executions, Advocates were used to spread the message. Results were extremely powerful.

Our agency created a series of films that pushed the limits of performance, specifically with the intention of sparking discussion and creating dialogue around the BMW 1 Series M Coupé. The first film was entitled *Walls* and showcased the 1M's unbelievable precision-driving capabilities as it sped through a series of silhouette cutouts in concrete walls. The second film, *Helipad*, featured the 1M drifting atop the world highest helipad (Figure 3.6). Both pushed the limits, were thrilling and fun to watch, and delivered on high performance. To watch videos, go to BMW M-Powered Films: http://cundari.com/cases/bmw-m-powered-films.

We accessed out-of-home media, cinema, and rich online banners to drive traffic to YouTube. Our results were immediate; the conversation was ignited. Advocates took the discussion further, analyzing the films and posting their points of view on every film

BMW 1M Walls   *BMW 1M Helipad*

Figure 3.6   BMW films that push the limit.

Without prompting, an Advocate created his own video game.

Figure 3.7   Advocate-created content.

segment. Some even added their own soundtracks and created their own video games using the 1M manoeuvring through the walls (Figure 3.7).

Coverage from the marketing and automotive press was overwhelming, and it soon spilled over into mainstream media. After just two days, *Walls* was the most viewed, top-favorite, and commented on automotive video on YouTube, and within a month, the films had reached over 6 million combined views. To further fuel the discussion, we leaked behind-the-scenes footage.

The results were staggering: to date over 6.9 million online views, 575,800-plus YouTube comments, Facebook shares, tweets, blog posts, and news mentions. Best of all, following the launch of the campaign were three successive months of record-breaking sales in the history of BMW Canada (up 17 percent from the same month the year before).

The program's success received international recognition and was judged the top-ranked program in the WARC 100, The World's Smartest Campaigns. WARC compiled and analyzed the top global ad effectiveness and strategy competitions, and used those results to rank programs from around the world.

Achieving these results once can be considered an anomaly, but repeating and improving these results each year for consecutive new product launches indicates that there is more at work here than just a great campaign.

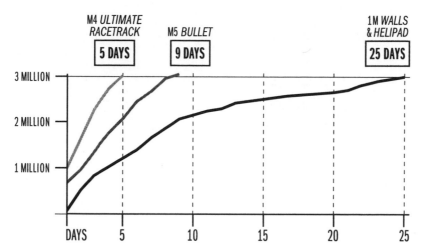

Figure 3.8   The race to 3 million views.

As a way of demonstrating this, with each new release, in 2011 (1M *Walls* and *Helipad*), 2012 (M5 *Bullet High Performance Art*), and 2014 (M4 *Ultimate Racetrack*), the time needed to reach the 3-million-view benchmark has shortened. While the 1M videos took a combined 25 days, the M5 and M4 videos needed only 9 and 5 days, respectively (see Figure 3.8).

When marketers say Advocates are worth more than their weight in gold, they're right! That means we're obligated to constantly provide exceptional value in content that exceeds Advocates' expectations to keep them truly engaged and supporting our brands.

CHAPTER FOUR

FROM FUNNEL TO THE JOURNEY

The New Customer Purchase Journey

As we've discussed, the age of the consumer has laid the foundation for a new brand-customer dynamic, and marketers have little choice but to adapt. Building and sustaining a customer-dominant relationship depends on creating engaging, relevant, customer-centric experiences—from initial awareness to post-purchase—at every point along the customer purchase journey.

So it's not surprising that these new relationships are translating into a shift in customer purchasing behavior. What used to be a linear process is now a nonlinear journey with a lot of side trips along the way. The traditional marketing and sales process, affectionately known as the funnel, was made up of four stages: awareness, interest, desire, and action. In practice, the brand would use some form of disruptive communication or stimulus to create awareness so that the top of the funnel would fill with potential customers. Once in the funnel, customers would evaluate the offering and proceed through the various stages or touchpoints, with some dropping out along the way, until the remaining customers fell to the bottom and bought the product. It was very linear, and marketers could assign some level of predictability to each stage of the process and ultimate outcome. One of the reasons direct marketing became very effective then was that marketers could see where they were losing prospects, tweak their tactics or messaging, and determine which offer combinations were most persuasive in moving prospects through the funnel to purchase. In this world, brands had complete control over the touchpoints; today, however, the purchase journey is a very different story.

We are witnessing a customer decision-making process that has evolved into a fluid, customer-controlled journey. While it still travels through a variety of stages, each step is now influenced by multiple factors. Before we distill each of these steps and examine them in detail, a note of caution is needed.

Many marketing pundits, with good research and proven track records, are happy to share their take on "new" customer purchasing behavior . . . but beware. They're often saddled with some "old school" characteristics, particularly in how they interact with customers. For many brands, the interaction (e.g., correct content at the right time) is still based on their perspective and not the customer's. So, while they correctly identify the journey stages from awareness, to research and consideration, to evaluation, to purchase and experience, they are still stuck looking at behavior from only the marketer's point of view.

To update the funnel approach, we need to make the entire journey more customer centric. I looked at and combined several models, edited out old thinking, and added new insights to create a comprehensive customer-focused snapshot of the new Customer Purchase Journey.

Here's how I built the twenty-first-century model of customer behavior.

MODEL 1. THE CUSTOMER DECISION JOURNEY

I began by reviewing the CDJ—"Customer Decision Journey"—which is based on exhaustive global research into how people buy products and services. Findings revealed that connected customers, who are dealing with the explosion of new digital channels, technologies, and products, have changed their purchasing behavior in significant ways.[1] This new behavior has led to the development of the CDJ model, which consists of five stages:

1. Initial consideration
2. Active evaluation
3. Moment of purchase
4. Postpurchase experience
5. Loyalty loop

Compared against the traditional sales funnel, the CDJ delivers three major improvements and insights:

1. *Brand consideration:* In the initial consideration stage, customers have a predetermined set of brands on their shopping list, so to get on the list, brand awareness matters. However, as they begin the evaluation phase and collect more information, they may expand their considered list of brands instead of reducing it, which is how the old sales funnel has worked.

2. *Empowered customers:* Customers now control the process and pull in information based on their need and stage in decision making. They don't rely on the marketer, especially as a single source, to provide them with information. Research findings show that *two-thirds of the touchpoints* in the evaluation stage *are customer driven.*

3. *Two types of loyalty, not one:* Providing postpurchase support to encourage or maintain loyalty is not a new concept, but in the CDJ model, not all loyalty is created equal. Results indicate there are active loyalists (we prefer Advocates), who stick with the brand and actively recommend it, and there are passive loyalists, who are loyal until something better comes along.[2] With six times more passive loyalists than active loyalists, we need to make sure they don't get distracted by competitive offers. Both are extremely valuable customers, some of our most valuable assets, but each requires different treatment.

MODEL 2. FROM DECISION POiNTS TO MOMENTS OF TRUTH

I next explored the Procter & Gamble (P&G) model, "Moments of Truth," created in 2005. Simply put, P&G believes two decision points determine a brand's success: the First Moment of Truth (FMOT) and the Second Moment of Truth (SMOT).[3]

FMOT occurs when a customer walks into a store, picks a brand off the shelf (this brand instead of that one), and takes it home. SMOT occurs when the customer uses the brand at home and has either a good experience or a bad one. P&G believes that, if a brand wins at both of these moments, the probability of a repeat purchase is high.

MODEL 3. ZERO MOMENT OF TRUTH

Over the last couple of decades, touchpoints have been the rallying cry of integrated marketers. However, up until now, the brand did most of the touching, and the customer not so much. Today, customers are touching (maybe pushing back is more accurate). So brands have to recognize and be cautious about how they contact and interact with customers. This new dynamic is demonstrated in Google's Zero Moment of Truth (ZMOT), the third model that I studied.[4]

ZMOT can be thought of as prestep to P&G's model, adding the moment a customer first receives a stimulus to FMOT and SMOT. As a result, customers become aware of the product or service and begin learning more about it by using their preferred digital devices. By the time they go to a store, pick up a phone, or order online (FMOT), they are incredibly well informed. They have input from friends, third-party ratings and reviews, videos, search results, brand websites, traditional media, and more. Not surprisingly, there is a high probability that, as a result of this research, customers will add other brands to their consideration list, as well as remove some of their initial preferences.

As part of the ZMOT validation process, a study of 5,000 shoppers was conducted across 12 categories to gain insights on customer decision making. One finding was that the average shopper used *10.4 sources of information* to make a decision in 2011, up from 5.3 sources in 2010.[5] The study also revealed that 84 percent of shoppers said their final decision was shaped by the research they did in the ZMOT phase.

As Bob Thacker, former OfficeMax CMO, notes:

> *Engagement with the customer today isn't just pouring a message down on their head, hoping they get wet. It's about really understanding that you must be present in a conversation when they want it, not when you want to. Pre-shopping before buying has become a huge part of customer behavior. In the past, it was pretty much confined to big-ticket items like cars or expensive electronics or homes. Now people engage in discovery before shopping on very small things.*

The findings reinforce the obvious: There aren't any information barriers anymore. Whether surfing the Web while waiting for the bus, browsing in-store, or sitting in a coffee shop with some form of screen in hand, customers have unlimited access to information anytime, anywhere. So you have to ask yourself: "What will they find when they start their journey with my brand? Do we understand their needs and give them the information they want? Is my content static or dynamic and entertaining? Does it work seamlessly on every platform? Can they personalize their experience? Can they find links to third-party experts, customer Advocates, or community forums? How easy is it to find us—do we have the right search engine optimization (SEO) strategy in place?"

All of the preceding considerations are important, because any negative experiences will be shared through their social media channels. And comments don't vanish into the digital ether; instead, they live on and on in the never-closed digital archive, where they remain available today, tomorrow, and every day after that.

THE NEW MODEL: CUSTOMER PURCHASE JOURNEY

By combining elements from CDJ, FMOT+SMOT, and ZMOT and adding our own proprietary Advocate Influencer Loop, we created the Customer Purchase Journey model (see Figure 4.1).[6] It's designed to capture the nonlinear customer-buying process and incorporate multiple touchpoints and feedback loops into a holistic customer-centric model. And we also sought to leverage the Advocate's impact on the buying process. Let's take a closer look at this model.

THE ADVOCATE AND INFLUENCER LOOP

As discussed earlier, Advocates have a disproportionate impact on brand reputation and revenues by spreading messages and content that influence others and accelerate their buying process. By actively promoting the brand and its benefits to customers and prospects alike, Advocates are more powerful than any messaging the brand does by itself, and they are an asset worth protecting.

CUSTOMER PURCHASE JOURNEY

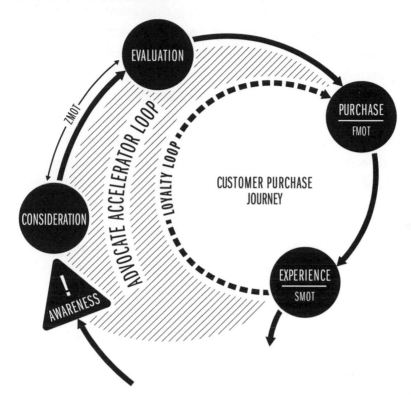

Figure 4.1   Customer Purchase Journey and Advocate Accelerator Loop.

FMOT = First Moment of Truth: what people think when they see your product and the impressions they form when they read the words describing your product.

SMOT = Second Moment of Truth: what people think, feel, see, hear, touch, and taste as they experience your product over time. It's also how the company supports them.

ZMOT = Zero Moment of Truth: what people search and find after getting their first stimulus.

And so it's obvious that Advocates need to be part of the new marketing model. Their inventory of perceptions/opinions has a direct influence on the intent-to-purchase and reputation of your product or brand. It could be a simple "comment" or an in-depth video post, but regardless, all content related to your brand becomes embedded in the journey and available for future customers.

The best high-quality customer content creates a special layer of opinion and knowledge, which we call the Advocate Accelerator Loop. Advocates are more than brand evangelists; they have become sharecasters who, when given the correct content tools, reshape and spread your brand through social media, which accelerates preference and influences others. They will also be staunch defenders of your brand when it is attacked. Their content has a major impact on the health of your brand and creates a financial return we call the return on involvement (ROI) (more on this coming up).

Advocates generate financial benefits in two ways. First, when new customers start their journey at ZMOT and start scanning the digital word-of-mouth archive, Advocate comments have enormous influence on their willingness to pursue a relationship with your brand. Second, Advocates purchase a lot more product than other customers. Research done recently in Germany indicates that they may be responsible for almost 80 percent of purchases.[7] There is no disputing it—Advocates are the customers you want and need, and you must cultivate and support them at every stage of the relationship.

A NEW CUSTOMER ROI

Understanding new customer purchase behavior is one thing, but converting it into metrics that prove payback on your customer-centric programs is still somewhat of a challenge. We believe the metric of the future will be return on involvement, or ROI. It's a reevaluation of the old ROI that demonstrates customer decision making and purchasing behavior in the context of the customer's relationship with the brand.

The additional factors of loyalty and advocacy provide a new lens on program results, and the question is, how do we capture data that reflects and incorporates the customer's influence on our results?

DEFINITION OF *RETURN ON INVOLVEMENT*

Return on Involvement is a term that has been hovering around the industry with a variety of meanings—ROI even made it on the Mashable 2013 buzzword list.

Given the dynamic changes in the purchase journey and customer–brand interaction, it's critical that we tie these factors back to sales for determining the ultimate success of our brand. In this way, the Return on Involvement measurement does not replace existing key performance indicators (KPIs) but, rather, supplements and enhances their current reporting and value. For example, the net promoter score is a great KPI that effectively measures the strength and relevance of a brand by determining how likely users are to recommend it to others. In this KPI, recommenders can be broken into three groups: *promoters* who are loyal enthusiasts and will keep buying and referring others; *passives* who are satisfied but unenthusiastic or neutral customers who are vulnerable to competitive offers; and *detractors* who are unhappy customers who can damage your brand through their negative word of mouth.

Other important and useful existing metrics include e-commerce transactional data, customer tracking conversion optimization, cost per sale, cost per lead, customer value, and traffic-to-lead ratio.

Regardless of what KPIs you use now, they should be providing you with simple but actionable outputs and benchmarks. Return on Involvement is no exception.

Here are simple and efficient ways you can begin to utilize ROI:

- Divide your marketing costs by total customer engagement (how many times all customers interact with your brand either on- or offline) to arrive at a percentage of cost per interaction.
- The next step is to divide incremental revenue by marketing costs to determine the incremental revenue percentage.
- The final step is to divide your cost per interaction by your incremental revenue percentage to produce the ROI metric.

THE RETURN ON INVOLVEMENT FORMULA

$$ROI = \frac{\text{Marketing Costs} \div \text{Total Customer Engagement} = \text{Cost Per Interaction}}{\text{Incremental Revenue} \div \text{Marketing Costs} = \text{Incremental Revenue \%}}$$

In this formula, there are three variables that drive final measurement:

1. Marketing spend
2. Total customer interactions
3. Incremental revenue

The goal is to outperform current benchmarks by producing outcomes that combine low marketing costs with high customer engagement—you'll produce higher incremental revenues along with better margins. The same ROI formula can be used to measure individual programs or compare one versus another. By looking at variables such as creative approach, media channel selection, or customer segments, results and learning can be transferred into future program planning.

Given the changes in the Customer Purchase Behavior Journey and the variables that are required to engage with and build loyal customers, you cannot simply measure results using yesterday's KPIs. You cannot measure new ideas using the measurement tools and analysis of the past; you will need to combine the best of the old with new analytical methods to produce reliable and consistent real-time outcomes, coupled with intuitive sensory decisions.

CHAPTER FIVE

BRANDS WILL NEVER BE THE SAME

Making Your Brand a "Beacon of Light"

FOR DECADES, MARKETERS HAVE BUILT THEIR BRANDS ON A fairly predictable playing field with a consistent set of rules. Until recently, it could be characterized as a somewhat one-sided affair, where marketers pushed their message out to the assembled customer masses. Before the Digital Age, traditional advertising and its mass delivery systems provided efficient, predictable, and safe channels for the delivery of brand messaging to customers.

As we've seen and discussed in previous chapters, customers now have a formidable decision-making role in a brand's future longevity. Empowered with technology and social media, customers are redefining how the game is played.

As Amazon's Jeff Bezos says, a brand is:

"The things that people say about you when you're out of the room."

Today, customers are saying a lot, and not just to their immediate social circle. They are talking to anybody and everybody online. And when they're not talking, they're listening to whoever else is talking to inform their brand perceptions. This role reversal has given customers a significant influence on the health and reputation of any brand.

DOES A BRAND ADD VALUE?

One could ask: "Are brands still relevant and valuable in today's marketplace?" My answer is a resounding "yes!"—brands are probably even more important than ever before, for in the sea of distraction surrounding today's customers, a brand can be "the beacon of light"—the one place with the ability to connect your product/service story and organizational values to customers as well as employees.

Strong brands add real, tangible value to any business. Jim Stengel, in his book *Grow*, puts some real meat on the bones of brand valuation. Here's one of his great illustrative points: In 1980, the entire market capitalization of the Standard & Poor's 500 consisted of tangible assets such as cash, offices, plants, equipment, and so on.[1] In 2010, tangible assets accounted for only 40 to 45 percent of these same companies' market cap; the rest were intangible assets, and about half of those assets, more than 30 percent of total capitalization, was attributed to the brand. Stengel also conducted a proprietary 10-year growth study of more than 50,000 brands around the world, with revealing results. Companies that reflected the principles of his "Grow" model, which uses "Brand Ideals" as its core business driver, achieved growth that was three or more times greater than their competitors'. He then took the top 50 companies in the study and created the Stengel 50. His findings showed that these 50 companies had generated a ROI that was 400 percent better than the Standard & Poor's 500. That is definitely not too shabby.

Stengel identifies the "Brand Ideal" as the key factor in building successful brands. The Brand Ideal is based on using one (or possibly two) of five human values from the following list—all of which focus on improving people's lives—as a guiding light for everything from operating structure to customer service to hiring. The companies that made up the Stengel 50 all had at least one of these human values:[2]

- *Eliciting joy:* Activating experiences of happiness, wonder, and limitless possibility. Stengel cited Coca-Cola, Zappos, and Moët & Chandon as examples.
- *Enabling connection:* Enhancing the ability for people to connect with one another and the world in meaningful ways, such as Starbucks, FedEx, and Natura.
- *Inspiring exploration:* Helping people explore new horizons and new experiences, such as Amazon.com, Apple, and Red Bull.
- *Evoking pride:* Giving people increased confidence, strength, security, and vitality, such as Hermès, Hugo Boss, and Mercedes-Benz.
- *Impacting society:* Affecting society broadly, including challenging the status quo and redefining categories, such as Dove, IBM, and Royal Canin.

ROI results of 400 percent over the S&P 500 is not only impressive but also speaks to a new lens that customers are using to choose a brand. Today's customers seek brands whose values are in sync with their own, and if the match isn't there, there are many other options they can choose from.

IF A BRAND HAS VALUE, WHAT ARE ITS VALUES?

Several leading brand thinkers have attempted to answer this question, and they share similar perspectives to my own. Let's take a look at what they have to say.

Simon Sinek talks about the Golden Circle, which consists of three interdependent variables, "Why, How, and What," as the platform for corporate inspiration.[3] Although he focuses more on leadership, Sinek's thinking has direct application to the creation of strong, customer-centric brands. The focus on "Why" refers to the organization's purpose, values, and beliefs—those areas that differentiate you from your competitors and have appeal to customers. "Why" defines why you do what you do. Understanding the "Why" of your organization goes to the core of your existence and acts as the primary force behind how your organization makes a positive contribution to a customer's life. Customers aren't that interested in "What" you do. "What or How" are essentially proof points that bring your organization's values or beliefs to light in a tangible way. It's the "Why" that connects customers to your brand on an emotional level.

Joey Reiman, whose experience includes managing global brands such as Coca-Cola and P&G, talks about "Purpose" as the defining force behind successful brands.[4] A business's purpose goes beyond the top and bottom lines to align with customer needs at a relationship level that exceeds product or service bonds. Brands that focus their efforts on a purpose that improves the lives of their customers have a golden opportunity to create strong and lasting relationships with those customers.

In today's marketing environment, product, service, and operational excellence are easily copied. The real point of advantage for a brand lies in the values to live by and how those values mesh with the needs and aspirations of their customers.

THEY'RE JUST NOT THAT INTO YOU

With this new thinking on how a brand connects with customers, it should be easy to create a strong brand, right? Hmmm, unfortunately, there may still be a few obstacles in your way. Let's go back to a brand's basic premise. As a marketer, you make a promise to deliver a product or service that meets the expectations of your customer. In turn, the customer trusts you to deliver on your promise and pays accordingly. As we've discussed, this arrangement worked pretty well for marketers up until the last decade. Since then, it's gone off the rails in a fairly dramatic way. As I mentioned earlier (Figure 3.2, Decline in brand trust), brand trust among customers has dramatically decreased, and the long-term outlook on repairing that damage is very problematic as customers shift to new sources of trust (friends, family, reviewers, etc.) when they evaluate a product or service. When you combine the downward trend in brand trust with new customer behaviors, positioning your brand as trustworthy is tougher than ever before.

SO WHAT'S A BRAND SUPPOSED TO DO?

In the new marketing landscape, customers don't really trust brands or want to talk to them, and they could care less about your branded content on- or offline—unless it has real value for them. Marketers have hoped that social media would repair some of the relationship gap, but they haven't quite caught up with the shift in customer thinking. Research shows that 70 percent of CMOs believe their online customer interactions are about providing brand information and letting customers express an opinion, and that the combination of those initiatives creates the kind of experiences that will connect customers to their brand.[5] That's not how it's working, however. Most customers have a different objective. For them, this is a much more transactional experience—61 percent are looking for discounts, and 33 percent are making purchases. Only 33 percent are looking for the brand connection, at least for now.

Brand apathy is prevalent. Customers live in a saturated marketplace, and they are bombarded by brand messaging from the moment they open their eyes in the morning. It's not surprising that they tune you out and instead rely on friends, social media, and other resources to make buying decisions. Google estimates that they connect with an average of 10.4 different sources when considering making a purchase. For you to make a meaningful and welcome connection with customers at this or any stage of their decision journey is a perplexing challenge.

So how do you break through? Here's what Steve Jobs said on his return to Apple (leading to Apple's "Think Different" campaign in 1997): "For me, marketing is about values. This is a very noisy world, and we're not going to get a chance to get people to remember much about us. So, we have to be very clear what we want them to know about us." What Jobs said then is even more powerful now in today's message-saturated marketplace.

"A brand that stands for something more, something at the heart of the business, and something that resonates with customers has the potential to connect brand and customer in a meaningful, lasting way."

The establishment of a corporate ideal, purpose, or value can play an important internal role in unifying brand messaging across all customer touchpoints. By establishing a brand's core value across various media platforms, you also help set the framework for a consistent customer experience at every contact point. Talking to a brand is not on every customer's bucket list, but when they do, what most want is a simple, positive experience. If a brand can help them achieve their goals, the upside is a group of satisfied customers who spread the word of their experience through their on- and offline networks.

Another factor in creating superior customer experiences is ensuring that front-line, customer-facing employees buy into the brand value story and use it to guide customer interactions and relationships. Unfortunately, many organizations fail at this basic level of cultivating a brand-inspired, customer-centric culture. Forrester conducted research to evaluate this, and the results were less than inspiring. In an age when experiences rule, employees weren't getting the support they needed to provide excellent customer experiences. The study results indicated that employees faced four roadblocks that hampered their ability to provide superior, branded customer experiences.[6]

INCOMPLETE UNDERSTANDING OF BRAND ATTRIBUTES THAT SHOULD DRIVE THE CUSTOMER EXPERIENCE

Sixty percent of senior executives said their companies' brand attributes are well defined; however, only 41 percent believe that their employees fully understand those key attributes, and only 45 percent said that these brand attributes drive how their companies design their customer experience.

INCONSISTENT IMAGE OF TARGET CUSTOMER

While 60 percent of surveyed businesses said their companies have a clearly defined set of customers, only 24 percent of their employees have an understanding of who they are.

NO REWARD FOR IMPROVING CUSTOMER EXPERIENCE

Ninety percent of those surveyed said customer experience is a critical part of their corporate strategy, but only 31 percent recognize or reward employees for improving the customer experience.

POOR EXECUTIVE ROLE MODELS

Just over 50 percent of those surveyed say senior executives regularly communicate the importance of serving target customers. More shocking is the fact that only 40 percent of these same executives actually interact with customers on a regular basis.

These findings make one thing abundantly clear: A customer-centric culture starts at the top—it must be endorsed and enforced to make it work at the bottom where the heavy lifting takes place. It's easy to put customer centricity on a PowerPoint slide but not so easy to make it part of an organization's culture and day-to-day delivery without strong leadership.

The new customer behavior has serious implications for all brands. If organizations don't commit to meeting their customers' expectations today, customers will go elsewhere tomorrow. For businesses that are still working with a traditional mindset, being customer centric requires a complete overhaul and review of business activities from top to bottom to ensure that the entire staff is united behind the brand aspirations of the business.

SO, WHAT'S NEXT?

Although daunting, the rewards are significant for businesses that establish customer experience as a primary contributor to brand reputation. Core brand values provide much-needed direction for what is to happen at every customer interaction. This is important, because if your organization is filled with silos, each offering its own form of brand messaging and customer experience, then the inconsistencies add up, and your brand's reputation could be decimated. Businesses that channel their brand's values into a unified customer experience can expect positive returns on revenue and reputation.

The importance of brand consistency goes beyond touchpoints; it also establishes the right conditions for enterprise-wide collaboration. Different business units across the enterprise can more easily come together and work from the same brand narrative to craft and deploy programs. By reinforcing the brand promise or purpose across the units, you create an agile organization that is ready to deal with today's always-on marketplace. Strong brands share a common starting point for employees that allow them to react to customers or market demands with confidence and speed. Speed to market is one thing; getting there with the right "stuff" is what separates the winners from the losers.

So, hopefully, I've convinced you to accept the idea that your brand's strength originates in its ideals, values, and purpose. Your next step is to channel those attributes into a differentiated, profitable, and sustainable business. We're not talking about your operating competencies, because they can be copied and probably done cheaper. Even your intellectual property (IP) can be difficult to protect. What I'm suggesting is that your real differentiator—the one that many businesses neglect—is your organizational culture and the employees within it.

Think of this as "cultural competency," where competency is directly attributable to knowledge of the culture and everyone's commitment to it. This enterprise-wide commitment acts as a catalyst for collaboration across business units and embraces diverse skill sets that help foster innovative solutions. Conversely, isolated expertise limits corporate ability to produce innovation at the level required to survive in this business climate.

Here is one last thought about branding. You probably don't go a day without hearing about how "innovation is a key driver of success." And it's true: Successful brands in all categories embrace innovation as an essential part of their brand identity and organizational philosophy. But the truly successful brands realize that innovation doesn't come solely from R&D or from any one department, for that matter; it comes from all parts of your business. An organizational culture that encourages and supports innovation through the removal of silos and the continued growth of employee competencies holds the key to fulfilling the brand promise and meeting the needs of the customer. This becomes all the more obvious when I see customer-centric efforts failing because of the broken connection between employees, or between employees, the brand, and customers. Creating a culture that embraces and encourages innovation and collaboration is an invaluable asset and an important part of your brand's strength and identity.

So, how healthy is your brand? Take a moment and consider these questions. Even better, get your employees involved, too. You never know what you'll discover.

ASK YOURSELF THE FOLLOWING QUESTIONS

- Why does our company exist? What were the thoughts and motivations of the founders?
- How do our products/services meet the needs of our customers?
- What makes us stand apart from the competition?
- What is our brand's essence? What is its purpose? What values does it possess that support its purpose?
- What do our customers say about us?
- What do our employees say about us?
- What do our partners say about us?
- How is our company's brand presented to the marketplace? Are our brand message and visuals consistently displayed across all lines of business?
- Do we have a collaborative workplace where everyone is committed to and understands the brand, and how do those values show up in the customer experience?

TELUS TALKS BUSINESS CASE STUDY

The telecommunications (telco) business is probably one of the most challenging and competitive markets on the face of the planet. This is especially true when dealing with business customers, and TELUS, a client at the time was facing an immense challenge in attracting and retaining them. When we did a deep dive into the research, we began to appreciate how business customers felt overwhelmed by an ever-growing choice of options that were critical to success. Ultimately, customers want clarity, and to find it, they were going outside normal media and sales channels into social media and community forums to find answers and insights from their peers.

The choice was either to ignore these forums or to participate in them—and even lead the discussion. We embraced the latter and launched an innovative social and digital strategy designed to engage customers and encourage dialogue. The destination for this experience was telustalksbusiness.com (see Figure 5.1).

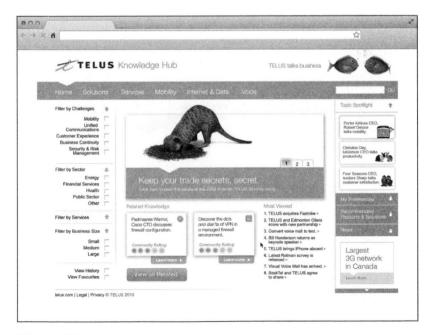

Figure 5.1   TELUS Talks Business Knowledge Hub.

Figure 5.2   Interactive out-of-home displays in airport lounges and high-traffic business district walkways.

In order to create a place for customers to come together, exchange ideas, and get expert advice, a totally new TELUS B2B social community site was required. This included a variety of traditional (see Figure 5.2 and 5.3) and digital initiatives that promoted the site, built traffic, and delivered a valuable experience to meet customers' specific and pressing needs.

To answer questions, the site was designed around dialogue and collaboration, and with that in mind, TELUS created a community where customers had easy access to information, peers, and experts. As part of the solution, we helped build a content engine that, based upon request, provided customers with relevant information. Then, using their request as a benchmark, related content was selected and pushed out in a strictly maintained "We're here to help you, not sell you" environment.

Figure 5.3   Print advertising to build awareness and drive traffic to telustalksbusiness.com.

TELUS Talks Business took off. In year one, the site showed a 1,200 percent increase in Web traffic from C-suite and IT management visitors, a 4,500 percent increase in lead generation, and an 8,000 percent increase in the sales close rate, with a 30 percent reduced cost per lead.

Even more interesting is that we built a unique filter into the site to track prospective customers and their requests. This intelligent scoring algorithm enabled progressive profiling, allowing the right messages to be delivered to the right audiences at the right time. It enabled us to track visitors and progressively score them as marketing qualified leads (MQLs) as they moved through the site. Again, sales discussions only happened at the request of the customer. In a market segment, where gains are hard to come by, we saw the program produce remarkable growth in both business results and differentiation.

The TELUS team realized outstanding improvements in results from defining its lead-to-revenue taxonomy.

- Most organizations would be happy with doubling their close rate; the TELUS team experienced an eightfold increase in its sales close rate.
- Unactioned leads dropped to 8.8 percent and was attributed to the use of lead scoring, which helped prioritize the work and increased sales' understanding of the value of the lead.
- The cost per lead was reduced by 30 percent, attributed to the efficiency gained through the use of marketing automation (MA) and the use of social media to create an inbound flow of leads.
- The marketing-sourced pipeline grew from the lead-to-revenue approach and the implementation of MA technology, which increased its marketing-sourced pipeline goal threefold.

At the core of this case study is the desire to provide a transparent flow of rich content resources from industry thought leaders, in-house experts, and peers to help telco business customers solve their problems. This is a great example of how an effective customer-centric approach can result in success on many levels, including sales.

CHAPTER SIX

CUSTOMER EXPERIENCE STRATEGY

Building a Customer Experience Organization

ON JULY 20, 1969, A HISTORICALLY SIGNIFICANT EVENT TOOK place that changed for me what I believed were humanity's boundaries and abilities. Though I was only 10 years old, this historic moment fully opened my eyes to what we are able to accomplish when we set a goal and put our mind to it. That event was the NASA space program and Neil Armstrong's first step on the moon.

Later on in life I was to learn a second lesson from that same profound event—one which continues to guide me to this day. I believe the journey to the moon, and not the event itself, provides us with insights into how we can steer ourselves through these turbulent times of hyper-speed change.

Even with a clear strategy and objective—*land a man on the moon*—and massive amounts of research and testing, the percentage of time that the space capsule was precisely on target during its flight was a mere 3 percent. In other words, that means the capsule was off course for 97 percent of the flight. Can you imagine what Neil Armstrong thought when NASA told him that he would be off target 97 percent of the time after liftoff?

However, astronauts are trained to manage through adversity, so accepting that course correction is the norm helped to focus and guide Neil and company during their voyage to achieve their goal.

I like to use the 97 percent rule to describe how we can maneuver through the constant customer changes in our marketplace. The only strategic constant is that we have to *constantly course-correct* to stay connected with our customers and achieve our objectives.

We have a good idea of what the new customers want and how they buy. During their purchase journey, they interact with a variety of influencers and influences pre- and postpurchase. They have friends, families, social networks, and Web-based third parties to provide information and guidance. On the other side, there is you, your brand, and your competitors' brands. But unlike the customer's circle of influencers, who are available on request, your brand has to fight through the cacophony and be ready for any request at any time from every touchpoint. Applying the 97 percent rule allows you to maneuver and course-correct to ensure that your customers get what they are looking for.

The availability, quality, and value of your content become the building blocks for your customers' experience. Your ability to match their needs with the appropriate message at the appropriate step in their journey becomes the crucial factor in whether you have a customer for life or a customer for a minute.

In fact, your ability to deliver is one of the few remaining competitive differentiators left to you. CMOs know that creating satisfied customers is one of their most important tasks. In a recent IBM study, 88 percent of CMOs made "getting closer to customers" their highest priority for the next 5 years.[1] There are many reasons for this, but the major one is the strong correlation between customer retention and profitability, as the following findings demonstrate:

- A 2 percent increase in customer retention has the same impact on profits as cutting costs by 10 percent.
- A 5 percent reduction in customer defection rates can increase profits by 25 to 125 percent, depending on the industry.
- Loyal customers are 15 times more likely to increase spending than high-risk intermittent customers.
- Repeat customers spend 67 percent more, on average.

The retention challenge for organizations is that customer loyalty is never a given. Attractive, competitive offerings are easily available, so keeping your customers loyal requires the commitment of everyone in your organization.

Customer experience has emerged as a leading factor in successful organizations because of the impact it has on all the elements of a business. There is a tendency to think "customer experience" has a stronger connection to the digital domain because of easily accessible analytical tools that track online customer behavior, but customer experience is incredibly important in offline environments, too. A more balanced framework is to approach marketing as an all- or omni-channel experience. This is especially relevant for retail operations. Remember, experiences don't occur in isolation; everything is interconnected in a customer's purchase journey. As a consequence, specific experiences can act as good or bad tipping points for the rest of the experience chain. It's the total experience your brand creates that determines the strength, resilience, and longevity of your customer relationships.

If you're thinking this all sounds like a lot of work, well, you're right. But first, I'd like to give you a suggestion: Simplify! When I'm faced with a complex problem and looking for gaps or opportunities, I think of "Occam's Razor," which is attributed to the fourteenth-century Franciscan friar William of Ockham. He came to the conclusion that when you're choosing between two competing theories, the simpler option is better than the complex one. The "Razor" in the title refers to the act of shaving off the complexities before you make your selection. With no shortage of complexity waiting for you, simplicity is a very important strategy to have in your back pocket.

Like it or not, digital technologies will continue to reshape our businesses and our lives. And since we're still in the initial stages of the Customer Age, who knows where technology will take us by 2020. For example, entire developing countries such as Uganda and Rwanda are leapfrogging earlier stages of development as they skip traditional telecom landline networks and go straight to mobile networks. As this trend continues, content, delivery platforms, and interfaces will need to accommodate the experiential needs of the many diverse customers who now interact with your brand. And in this scenario, simplifying your customer experience initiatives is a good way to keep you and your brand on track.

WHERE DOES CUSTOMER EXPERIENCE START?

Where do we begin to influence the customer? It seems like an overwhelming task and an octopus-like situation. I suggest that you start small and go for some low-hanging fruit and early wins. To do this, first break down every stage of the customer purchase journey for your product or service and then, within each stage, note every point of contact with the customer. At each point, see how customers could be interacting with the brand and where your brand fits into their decision-making process. In all likelihood, this will be a fairly complex system that includes employees, partners (outsourced call centers, technical services, etc.), various branded and nonbranded content sources, operating processes, and external influencers whom your customers trust.

By understanding this interconnected system, you'll start to see where the most important connecting "moments" are and what kind of content you need to provide customers at those given moments.

Once you start digging, opportunities to improve performance at individual touchpoints will begin to show themselves. It could be as simple as making an online form easier to fill out, improving website navigation based on past visits, or ensuring customer-facing employees have the right training to deal with customers. With these kinds of analytics, you can then prioritize your efforts and budget resources. Make sure you set up benchmarks to track and evaluate performance at each touchpoint to determine if your early initiatives are paying off. Once you have these initiatives going, they often lead to other insights and improvements. Before you know it, you'll be on the way to a truly customer-centric experience.

CENTER STRATEGIES ON CUSTOMER PERSPECTIVES

Successfully creating compelling customer content and experiences depends on your ability to capture actionable customer insights. To do this, you need an ongoing commitment to acquire the kind of knowledge that will improve your customers' experience and relationship with your brand.

The quest for customer insights is an organizational imperative. Most businesses actively engage in a myriad of activities to keep abreast of customer changes: monitoring complaints or service calls; listening to and tracking social media behavior; conducting ethnographic, usability, and customer satisfaction studies; and using customer enterprise data to analyze past behaviors and predict future behaviors, as well as gleaning insights from employees.

This is not an exhaustive list; it comprises the basics that businesses need to refresh the knowledge that will keep their customer-centric framework up to date. They must ensure their brand values are consistently being communicated and their product offering is meeting the needs of today's customers. Good customer experiences do not happen by accident.

NOT STRATEGY AS USUAL

So far we've looked at building customer experiences by studying and understanding their behavior through an organizational lens. But how about getting the customer directly involved in decision making and strategy development? We've started to see a movement among forward-thinking companies that invites customers to contribute input into the design of new products or services, even bringing them to a seat at the strategy-planning table.

There are two of reasons for this phenomenon. The first is that smart companies want to harness the power of social media and the innovative thinking coming from sources outside their business. The second is that Gen Y (those born in the late 1970s to the early 1980s) have come into the workplace with very different perceptions and behaviors. They see work as a nonhierarchal community, where workplace collaboration is a defining value, and assume their involvement will be welcome at all levels of the business.

MAKING TRANSFORMATION HAPPEN

It's one thing to talk about it, but it's another thing entirely to make it happen. A lot of organizations struggle to adapt to this new environment, and we're no different. I spent the last five years reinventing, retooling, and reorganizing Cundari Group Ltd. so that our teams can connect with this new customer. It hasn't been easy, but we did it, and you can, too—and it's exciting when everyone on staff gets involved, including clients and partners.

If you're already collecting and tracking customer behavior through your involvement with digital media, you'll find many of these lessons have application in nondigital media as well. Furthermore, offline activities have one key element that digital media don't have: real people. Customers may have good memories of a Web experience, but that will not resonate stronger than a really helpful personal experience that only a great customer representative can provide. Think about your own experiences with companies that are known for excellent personal service—how impressed you were and how special it made you feel. You'll remember these personal interactions far longer than recalling how many clicks it took you to check out on Amazon.com.

According to Forrester Research, positive experiences can be simplified and categorized into three key areas: Was it enjoyable? Was it easy? Was it useful?[2] These questions have direct application in any medium or situation, regardless of whether it's off- or online.

BREAKING NEW GROUND

To make it easier for you to get started on customer centricity in your organization, I'd like to provide a blueprint—a basic marketing model approach—that can help. Your speed of evolution will depend on a couple of things: where you are on the customer-centric curve now, how ready your organization is to accept change, and whether your operating structure can handle the requirements of a customer-centric business model (see Figure 6.1).

In our blueprint, we use a modular and interdependent structure that you can personalize; it is quite flexible and adaptable in any environment. The model has three integrated activity areas with the following goals:

1. *Customer centricity:* Understand customer needs, behaviors, and preferences.
2. *Marketing management:* Create, implement, and adapt processes and programs to deliver on customer needs.
3. *Marketing science:* Measure transactions and interactions across all customer journey touchpoints and capture quantitative evidence of your success and failures.

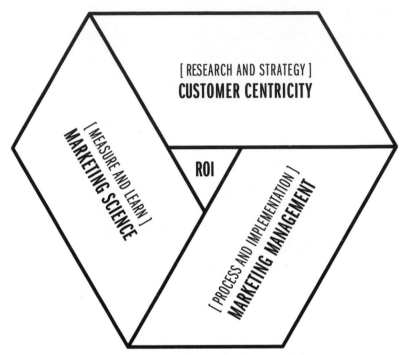

Figure 6.1   Customer-centric marketing model.

When you put together the elements, it looks like this

When combined, these three areas create a marketing ecosystem that encourages constant interaction and growth. And where they overlap, we call that the sweet spot—the Return on Involvement (ROI). Each subsystem comes together to create positive experiences, strong brands, loyal customers, and a healthy bottom line. Let's drill down and take a closer look at how these activity-marketing modules work together.

CUSTOMER CENTRICITY

In 2004, IBM's Global C-suite Study revealed that CEOs ranked customers sixth among those factors that they believed would drive organizational change.[3] Fast-forward to 2013, and customers are now ranked first! Customer centricity, and its associated disciplines, have become the foundation for business strategy; it shifts the acquisition of customer knowledge from a periodic activity (e.g., quarterly satisfaction studies) to a 24/7 undertaking. As a consequence, we require a high level of organizational dedication to ensure customer research is continually executed and, even more importantly, that any insights or learnings are transformed into action.

Your research department is essentially the custodian of your customers and all that they do. It could be a department of one—or, more realistically, a team whose members each have a different expertise: research design, implementation, interpretation, and distribution of the results to marketing and the rest of the organization.

With research, there are three areas I suggest you focus on to create better customer experiences: external initiatives, internal programs, and touchpoint knowledge. Here are the specifics.

EXTERNAL INITIATIVES

Research in this area shows that you should seek to learn as much as possible about the customer. This team is charged with projects such as:

- Ethnographic research
- Quantitative and qualitative research
- Online customer panels
- Designated customer fan groups
- Social media listening and watching
- Trend analysis
- Purchase history

INTERNAL PROGRAMS

Front-line employees are an excellent source of customer knowledge and can provide real insight on the state of the brand-customer relationship. Using qualitative and quantitative tools, employees can add valuable data to your customer knowledge bank. There is a high level of customer empathy, as these employees interact with customers in real time. They are the first to be aware of any developments (positive or negative) in the field. These internal groups include:

- Sales force
- Distribution
- Retail sales
- Channel members
- Customer service
- Technical support
- Call center
- Partners

TOUCHPOINT KNOWLEDGE

Touchpoints have taken on new importance as the customer journey has become increasingly complex, experiential, and nonlinear. For businesses to succeed, understanding customer experience at each milestone is necessary. Two areas of focus include:

- Customer experience in both online and offline environments
- Usability research on all screens and platforms

When you pull together lessons from all three of these sources, it's critical that you put them into an easy-to-access format that all business units can tap into.

MARKETING MANAGEMENT—PROCESS AND IMPLEMENTATION

The marketing team's responsibility is to convert customer knowledge into marketing programs that align with operations. That's why it's such an advantage to house data and analysis of customer knowledge inside the organization. By keeping this valuable asset in-house, you not only streamline your time-to-market but also ensure a consistent message. Here are some of the marketing programs that can be created from customer-centric data and analysis:

- Establishing the brand's values and how they act as key links between all business model elements
- Developing content that ensures that the brand's key messaging and visual elements are consistent across all screens, platforms, and media (especially when outside vendors are also involved)
- Designing content to work in different digital and offline environments
- Creating seamless transitions between channels for customers
- Putting governance policies in place to cover all aspects of the marketing mix
- Creating tools, processes, and governance that guide the entire organization in providing the right, consistent experience to customers
- Determining priority touchpoints and how to fund/invest in each of them accordingly
- Collecting and retaining customer data
- Developing intuitive analytics that are actionable across the organization

These are just some of marketing management's key responsibilities. I say "some," because in this unpredictable and shifting environment, it's entirely possible that your priorities will change tomorrow. To weather these changes and continue to succeed, you have to listen, understand, and respond to your customer in real time—and the best way to do that is to have the in-house expertise and capabilities that enable you to respond and adapt to changing circumstances. And remember the 97 percent rule.

MARKETING SCIENCE—MEASURE AND LEARN

Marketing science is concerned with business performance and operational analytics—the big-data side of the analytic puzzle. In your organization, it may be housed in the research department or another unit, but wherever it rests, it must be closely aligned to the customer-centric teams to ensure that they're focused on the business's strategic priorities. This is a great time to be a CMO, because you can now go into the C-suite with lots of performance numbers to prove the effectiveness of your programs. Conversely, it's a bad time to be CMO, because there is so much data that it's hard to know where to start.

Big data has been hailed as the Second Coming, but how to manage and use it is still a bit of a dilemma. If you're not part of the Fortune 500 club, it's a pricey proposition and a steep learning curve; however, there are some major changes that make it accessible and understandable for even the smallest companies. That's why I predict the emerging trend of "small data" will really take off, as smaller, more applicable data sets become available and more actionable for all companies to use.

For both big and small data, the challenge is that data without the correct lens, filter, or interpretation does not provide the answers. It's the garbage in/garbage out scenario. While it's important to know how customers search, how they purchase, how much they buy, how frequently they buy, and so forth, that doesn't necessarily tell you if they're having a good or bad experience. Experience is the key driver of sustainable loyalty. That's why you have to marry your quantitative data with qualitative, behavioral findings to truly understand what's happening—how sales metrics and experiences intersect to create sales and recommendations.

It's very easy to get distracted by big shiny data objects—so keep it simple. By framing your objectives, you'll be able to drill down to reach that elusive low-hanging fruit everyone talks about (but that is sometimes hard to grab). Avinash Kaushik, Google's analytics guru, talks about the importance of micro and macro outcomes, and how tackling the micro first lets you build credibility and confidence with the C-suite and the rest of the organization as well. For example, if the data demonstrates that an e-commerce ordering process is inefficient, and you solve the problem with a simple navigation fix that improves business flow and saves money, then you have a good story to tell. From that "simple is good" perspective, Kaushik outlines three areas of priority on which to focus your data-collecting efforts. They give you a chance to create specific, measurable micro outcomes.[4]

Acquisition: How are you anticipating acquiring traffic for your website, YouTube video, or whatever else you are creating? Did you cover all three components of successful acquisition: earned, owned, and paid media? How would you prioritize each? Where are you spending most of your efforts?

Behavior: What is the behavior you are expecting when people arrive? What pages should they see? What videos should they watch? Should they visit repeatedly? Are there certain actions they should take? What is unique about your effort that ties into an optimal experience for a customer?

Outcomes: What outcomes signify value delivered to the business bottom line? A download? A phone call to your call center? A qualified online lead? People signing up for e-mail promotions? People buying your product/services? A 95 percent task completion rate? A 10-point bump in brand perception?

With these three strategic data priorities, you can build your business goals and desired outcomes for each touchpoint using the following guidelines:[5]

- Create business objectives and supporting key performance indicators for all projects.

- Establish ROI models that reflect objectives and key performance indicators.
- Build the analytic capability in order to evaluate activities at each touchpoint.
- Identify the segments of people, behavior, and outcomes for analysis in order to understand why we succeed or fail.
- Measure touchpoint performance results against business metrics.
- Compile results and use them to develop a customer experience framework.

If you are just getting your feet wet, and/or budget is a concern, there are some good free analytics packages available, as well as inexpensive options for social media. Of course, there is no shortage of vendors to choose from.

The intent of this model is to create a business architecture where each operating unit is customer centric and experience focused. The commitment to satisfy customer needs through exceptional experiences at each stage of the decision journey will bond units together with this common goal—and will produce a sustainable and profitable return on involvement.

CHAPTER SEVEN

BUILDING RELATIONSHIPS WITH THE ADVOCATE/SHARECASTER

Creating Content

IN PREVIOUS CHAPTERS, WE'VE LOOKED AT FACTORS THAT DEFINE the new marketing environment and the powerful role that customers now play in the marketing ecosystem. In addition to new customer behaviors, you've seen how customer experience plays a pivotal role in the decision-making process and how brands provide the glue that binds all elements together to build strong relationships. To build these relationships, the primary currency is content, but it can't just be any kind of content. Like currency, it has to be valued by the customer, and its perceived value is directly related to how helpful, entertaining, and memorable the experience is to the customer.

"It's not what you say but how you make them feel."

Despite a limited attention span, customers have an insatiable need for content, not only to read, but also to share. Your customers now spend one hour and twenty-one minutes more per day consuming media than they did 10 years ago and, as previously discussed, rely heavily on the web when making a purchasing decision. But these are not passive audiences; they're engaged and selective. So, when your customers are evaluating content to help frame their purchasing decisions, whom do they trust? They seek out the small segment of family, friends, and your brand Advocates, who essentially become broadcasters or, in today's language, sharecasters, who are receiving, combining, creating, reviewing, and redistributing knowledge and advice on your brand's behalf.

The importance of this Advocate group to your brand is demonstrated in Forrester's 2013 North American Technographics Survey.[1] When asked "To what extent do you trust each of the following types of advertising/promotion?" this is how customers responded:

Brand/product recommendations from friends and family	70%
Professionally written online reviews	55%
Customer-written online reviews	46%
Natural search engine results	43%
Information on websites of companies or brands	32%
Sponsored search engine results	27%
E-mails from companies or brands	18%
Posts by companies or brands on social media sites	15%
Information on mobile applications from companies or brands	12%
Ads on websites	10%
Text messages from companies from brands	9%

The results clearly show that all content is not created equal and customers overwhelmingly prefer to pull information from sources they consider trustworthy. As soon as you move into branded, pushy messaging, trust levels decrease in a hurry.

WHY DO CUSTOMERS SHARE CONTENT?

When an Advocate/Sharecaster (A/S) shares your content or promotes your brand in the form of a review, video, blog, or other digital format, the assumption is that the A/S can be trusted and, by association, the brand can be trusted, too. As a consequence, having your content shared helps generate organic buzz and sales, so understanding why customers sometimes share and sometimes don't is vitally important. It's one thing for you to share content with a friend; it's another thing to have an A/S promote your brand and content to his or her network. Both are good, as they both convey a sense of trust, but the A/S will reach more people, with a high probability that those people will pass the content on to members of their social network. That's why it is so important to build content with the intention of its being shared, so it has value to the next user in the social network chain. To get there, brands have to empathize with the needs of both the A/S and the people in their social community. Customers share content for a variety of reasons, and a recent study outlined why:[2]

- 73 percent say they process information more deeply and thoughtfully when they share it.
- 85 percent say reading other people's responses helps them understand and process information and events.
- 94 percent carefully consider how the information they share will be useful to others.
- 49 percent say sharing allows them to inform others of products they care about and potentially change opinions or encourage action.
- 68 percent share to give people a better sense of who they are and what they care about.

To put it in the words of the customer:

> *"I remember products and information sources better when I share them and am more likely to use them."*

> *"I try to share only information that will reinforce the image I'd like to present: thoughtful, reasoned, kind, interested, and passionate about certain things."*

"One of the most powerful insights emerging from this study was that trust is the cost of entry for getting content shared —a great reminder for any business!"

Getting people to share information requires a delicate balance between the brand, content, customer, and Advocate. Not only do you have to maintain that balance; you also have to provide content that satisfies each stage of the customer decision journey.[3]

Creating content that encourages sharing and builds a genuine bond with your customers isn't easy. You can't just throw a fistful of content out there. To earn trust and loyalty, you need a useful and engaging story that resonates with their needs. It's a daunting task, so when you are creating new content, remember Occam's Razor; try to simplify the message by asking yourself three questions:

1. What can we do to meet the needs of our customer?
2. How does it match up with our business objectives?
3. Why is this consistent with our brand values?

ORGANIZATIONAL MIND-SET

I'd like to suggest that producing good content is not solely a marketing challenge—it's also an organizational challenge. For organizations that are not familiar with the demand for content, producing and distributing it in a timely manner can be challenging. Most businesses are still very hierarchal, which translates into slow decision making, and in our fast-moving marketplace, being slow can be a recipe for disaster. So, it's important to get senior executives' commitments up front, because without their buy-in, nothing is going to happen—or if it does happen without their support, the results may not match the best interests of the company. It's up to the senior executives to define the internal playing field, state who's in charge, and establish governance practices that guide content production throughout the organization. Their role is to ensure that consistency is a driving force in the content engine. Consistency takes shape in several areas:

- Timeliness in releasing content into the market.
- Quality (value) of the content message.
- Tone and manner are always consistent.
- The brand persona is consistently represented.
- Quality production values are always present.

In addition to senior leadership commitment, it's wise to add some publishing disciplines to your marketing communications toolbox that recognize content production demands. Also, remember that marketing can't be the only story provider; it's the responsibility of the entire organization. Think about all the different customer interactions happening across the organization and all the great things that employees are doing. They're all potential content story sources, and everyone across the organization should get involved to bring forward the stories that customers want to hear.

SLICED AND DICED DISTRIBUTION

Before you start to build or outsource your content capabilities, you need to consider that content does not fall into a "one size fits all" category. Sometimes it's specific to one medium (e.g., mobile phones) or more broadly applied, with the same content repurposed for different media. As a consequence, content can get sliced up in different ways, depending on your audience and the platform being used to distribute the content.

When you're planning your "content calendar," keep a high level of content flexibility to facilitate usage across all media options. Three key media channels should factor into your plan; each comes with its own audience, creative, and production considerations:

1. *Owned media:* These are the channels controlled/owned by your organization, such as websites, Facebook, Twitter, Pinterest, and so forth.

2. *Paid media:* These are the channels in which you pay to have your message appear, such as print and broadcast advertising in traditional and digital media.

3. *Earned media:* These media work when one customer passes on your content to another, based on a personal interaction with the brand. It could be a story reflecting a positive or negative experience or perhaps an interesting blog or Twitter link.

Owned and paid media have well-defined distribution paths for content and can be planned as part of a regular publishing schedule. Earned media is less predictable (and a double-edged sword) that depends on content quality, customer appeal, and shareability.

There's another form of content as well that I call *reactive publishing*. It includes activities such as responding to customer requests, correcting false perceptions, or participating in social media conversations. This can be a very powerful tool when used correctly.

MAKING THE CASE FOR DEMPSTER'S

Good content, created and used properly, can help build and strengthen relationships with your brand and act to counterbalance any negative or misleading messaging in the marketplace. When content is created and used properly, you can reduce negative or incorrect perceptions and build a new level of trust with your customers. To demonstrate, I'd like to show you some of the work that we did for our client Dempster's in a very low-interest category, bread.

THE DEMONIZATION OF BREAD

The popularity of low-carb and gluten-free diets has virtually demonized bread. These negative perceptions are also accompanied by increasing ingredient costs; all of this, combined, hit the bread market hard, resulting in customers buying a lot less bread products. In fact, over the last five years, the Canadian bread industry has seen sales revenues drop at an annualized 0.9 percent a year.

We believed that Dempster's needed to reframe the conversation that it was having with its customers, so we created a social media strategy that, in addition to its entertainment value, promoted and highlighted new products, encouraged consumption, and provided nutritional information. Several different executions, along with regular posts and discussions, were designed to entertain, engage, and deliver reassurance about bread's nutritional value.

REBUILDING BREAD

Research showed that deep down inside, Canadians love bread, but with all the gluten-free and low-carb hype, they had forgotten that bread provides healthy benefits such as fiber and vitamins like niacin, calcium, B_1, and zinc. We wanted to initiate a conversation to remind them, but how do you get people talking about the benefits of B_1, niacin, and calcium? The answer lay in a series of short, funny videos that entertained and also provided nutritional information.

STAR IN YOUR OWN SEXY ROMANCE NOVEL–THE LAUNCH OF ZERO BREAD

Building on the success of a previous campaign for Dempster's, we decided to connect with our key female audiences. Since bread-purchasing behavior spans multiple cohorts, we needed a story line that was engaging for all women. Our solution? Romance novels, since research showed 92 percent of all women read them.

We decided to take advantage of our target audience's guilty pleasure and align it with Dempster's Zero—a "good for you" bread with no added sugar or fat. Our message was that this product is not only good for you but also makes you feel sexy. We then gave customers a chance to star in their own personalized, full-length romance novel.

The campaign featured a sexy, shirtless cowboy (what else?) and invited viewers to click on his washboard abs—this took them to our Facebook app, where they could create, customize, and download their own romance novel, titled *Zero Inhibitions* (see Figure 7.1).

Viewers personalized their book by selecting their own name, eye color, hair color, and many other playful options, such as whether they liked bad boys or boy-next-door types.

We compiled the preferences into an original romance novel of over 135 pages, with over 30,000 words of customizable content, including alternate endings. Once complete, the custom book was downloadable to any e-reader or tablet.

Figure 7.1   *Zero Inhibitions* **personalized novel.**

Figure 7.2   Dempster's Zero bread promo video and innovative click on abs to get to *Zero Inhibitions* website.

To further support the campaign, we printed and bound customized copies and sent them directly to influential food bloggers.

The campaign resonated strongly and immediately—in the first two weeks alone, we had nearly 2,000 downloads. After one month, it was a third of the way to the top of the best seller list— and this one was *free*. VIDEO: Dempster's Zero Inhibitions: http://cundari.com/cases/dempsters-zero-inhibitions (Figure 7.2).

DIY SANDWICH EXPERT—LET'S HEAR IT FOR THE GUYS

Marketing campaigns for bread traditionally target moms, but research revealed an untapped and potentially profitable segment: sandwich lovers. Findings showed that Canadians are eating more sandwiches now than in the previous two years, but fewer make them themselves. In 2010, 64 percent of sandwiches were made at home, compared with 57 percent in 2012. The drop is primarily attributed to Millennial men who are buying their BLTs and Reubens at quick-serve restaurants.

We created video content that tapped into the DIY trend and spoofed popular home renovation shows like *Holmes Makes It Right*. We featured a sandwich-reno man, Butch, and his assistant, Jessica (Figure 7.3), helping a guy build an epic sandwich with tools that are

Figure 7.3   Butch and Jessica—sandwich renovators.

better suited to a garage workshop than a kitchen. We used a wood chipper for slicing lettuce and a blowtorch for toasting bread (you get the idea). Butch turned an amateur's sorry sandwich into a mouth-watering masterpiece. Also, while we were primarily targeting guys with this DIY spoof, the DIY trend has fairly universal appeal, so we were confident that women would chuckle at the video, too.

The spot lives on Dempster's YouTube page and is still running as a preroll (Figure 7.4). Display banner ads target male-specific

Figure 7.4   Jessica and the sandwich toolkit.

sites like sports networks, while the video and a microsite (http://diysandwich.ca) push viewers to an Instagram contest, where they can post photos of their mouth-watering creations using the hashtag #DIYsandwich.

Dempster's cross-promoted with brands offering sandwich fixings like cheese and deli meats, and placed their bread racks near those products to encourage customers to "Grab it. Build it. Eat it."
VIDEO: Dempster's DIY Sandwich: http://cundari.com/cases/dempsters-diy-sandwich
VISIT: Dempster's DIY Sandwich ideas: http://www.diysandwich.ca

2-MINUTE MORNING QUICKIE

Breakfast is said to be the most important meal of the day, but alas, many of us tend to skip it, or worse, grab something that isn't very healthy. (I'm just guessing here.) Dempster's wanted to give breakfast eaters another option—one that was tasty, nutritious, and fast, so we created the *2-Minute Morning Quickie* and it was very straightforward (Figure 7.5).

The concept stems from the insight that Canadians love breakfast sandwiches but believe that they are difficult and time-consuming to prepare, so our messaging was direct—two minutes is all it takes! Dempster's English Muffins and Bagels

Figure 7.5   *2-Minute Morning Quickie*—the final product.

let customers indulge in a morning quickie . . . and make themselves a delicious breakfast sandwich that starts their day off right (Figure 7.6).

The *2-Minute Morning Quickie* video dispels the myth that making a breakfast sandwich is difficult by demonstrating a simple recipe. Through the use of innuendo, we connect with the target in a highly entertaining and informative way.

VIDEO: Dempster's 2-Morning Quickie: http://cundari.com/cases/dempsters-morning-quickie

Dempster's is a good example that when it comes to content, one size (or message) does not fit all. By using different stories, techniques, and media, we built a unique content curriculum that appeals to the different needs of different audiences. Having storylines that entertain and engage each customer type is key, as is ensuring that the product's unique benefits support and underscore the fun approach.

Social media and its assorted channels give you the opportunity to reach the customer on your own terms. But, and it's a big *but*, you have to acknowledge and respect the terms of your customers and customize your content with them in mind. I see the brand as a painting and your content as the brushstrokes, where every stroke is important in the composition of the final picture.

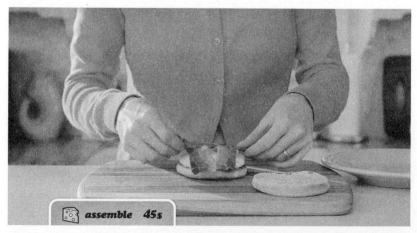

Figure 7.6   Instructions on creating the *2-Minute Morning Quickie*.

LISTENING IS AS IMPORTANT AS STORYTELLING: REAL-TIME MARKETING (RTM)

Up to this point, we've discussed building your content around a somewhat predetermined and proactive publishing strategy. We've demonstrated flexibility in tailoring your content based on audience needs, making sure it's available at the right time, placing it in your customers' journey, and enabling you to push it out on a schedule of your own making.

However, there is another form of content that's extremely important to your brand's success, and it revolves around what's called real-time marketing (RTM). As the name suggests, the customer initiates the interaction, and you have to be ready to respond in real time. RTM incorporates a wide range of activities, but for our purposes, let's look at RTM in the context of marketing communications, specifically in the context of social media. Opportunities for RTM occur when:

- Engaging directly with individuals on a one-to-one basis
- Interacting with your audience around a topic or event
- Most importantly, engaging the audience in the delivery of your brand's product or service in a way that differentiates you from the competition

The poster child for RTM is Nabisco's Oreo response to the 2013 Super Bowl blackout, which was extremely clever and memorable. When the stadium lights went out, they tweeted an ad that read: "Power out? No problem" with an image of a single Oreo and the caption: "You can still dunk in the dark." Oreo was prepared and had a 15-person team monitoring what was going on in the social environment and were able to decide on the spot what to do. Let's face it; this once-in-a-lifetime event could only have been possible because they were ready and understood the power of being relevant. There are many companies that took a page from Oreo's book, adopted RTM, and did a really good job.

CIBC FIFA WORLD CUP™ CANADIAN SPONSORSHIP

Through Visa's partnership with FIFA, CIBC was able to become the Official Canadian Bank in association with Visa of the 2014 FIFA World Cup™.

To put RTM into bigger context, we used RTM strategies on CIBC's 2014 FIFA World Cup Brazil™ sponsorship activation. To ensure that they got the most traction out of their sponsorship, we built a social campaign platform around the strategic theme: "There's a fan inside us all" to bring a seamless online-offline brand experience to fans across Canada.

Building on the energy of the FIFA World Cup, the CIBC team created social media content that was designed to encourage users to express their passion for the beautiful game and engage with CIBC and other fans through the online platform. The content strategy was built around three streams of messaging that included preplanned posts, preplanned promotional posts for Aventura (CIBC's travel rewards card portfolio), and real-time posts.

To ensure that we've stayed consistent and on strategy, we developed a social media moderation guide, crisis management guidelines, and a content strategy to govern the campaign. Also, for each content plan, we created content matrixes, common scenarios, and a library of responses.

We further focused our efforts by creating a social media war room in our agency to focus solely on managing CIBC's FIFA World Cup Social Community. The room was stocked with all of the hardware, software, and other resources needed to effectively manage the program. In addition, we staffed a CIBC Social Community Team (Figure 7.7) that was responsible for monitoring, moderating, and posting content 24/7 during key FIFA World Cup events during the 30-day competition. With a focus on listening, calibrating, and optimizing, we ensured that our content was relevant to fans engaging with the FIFA conversation online.

Figure 7.7   CIBC-dedicated FIFA World Cup™ war room.

Our content was so strong that we achieved click-through rates as high as 22 times the norm.

In a dedicated FIFA World Cup war room, a team of community managers and clients helped cultivate the CIBC community throughout the campaign and surprised and delighted loyal fans with FIFA World Cup–related goodies.

CONTENT DEVELOPMENT

The need for great content was relentless, and the team wrote and designed hundreds of preapproved CIBC social posts, which fit with our content matrix and messaging guidelines (see Figure 7.8). Planned content was augmented by real-time posts, which reflected what was happening in the community and on the field.

Real-time content was created in response to FIFA World Cup action and fan discussions and then was posted during matches to capture the excitement of the game and fuel conversation within our quickly growing and engaged community (see Figure 7.9). Our

Figure 7.8   Some of the hundreds of preapproved CIBC social posts.

creative teams utilized new Twitter functionality, and content reach was amplified through creatives that surprised and delighted.

FAN STANDINGS

To enable fans to share their passion for the FIFA World Cup and their favorite team, we developed a landing page on CIBC's sponsorship microsite called "Fan Standings." On the site, users could vote for their team via Twitter, using CIBC's unique hashtags, to determine

Figure 7.9   Real-time content was created in response to World Cup action.

Figure 7.10   CIBC's community hub, called "Fan Standings."

which FIFA World Cup team was most popular in each province. The website hub also aggregated CIBC's FIFA World Cup Twitter hashtags, to produce a live stream of tweets (see Figure 7.10).

SUPER FANS CONTEST

Surprise and delight was a huge component of our war room strategy. For every game, community managers were tasked with finding a fan of the match to reward. Fans were chosen based on the energy and frequency of their tweets, support of their team, usage of CIBC and FIFA World Cup hashtags and social clout. Once selected, they received a message from CIBC via Twitter to acknowledge their passion and spirit. After each big match, one "Super Fan" (see Figure 7.11) was selected by the CIBC team and sent an adidas brazuca official match ball of the 2014 FIFA World Cup or an Official Commemorative Coin of the 2014 FIFA World Cup Brazil. We had some great responses, as many fans shared their surprise at being selected along with images of their match ball on Twitter.

Figure 7.11   Fans active on Twitter were selected as Super Fans who shared their surprise at being selected.

RESULTS

The results outperformed all expectations and targets set for the programs. *Marketing* magazine ranked CIBC as the third most associated brand with 2014 FIFA World Cup Brazil on Twitter (following Adidas and Nike), beating out brands like Budweiser, Puma, and Coca-Cola. Holy Schnitzel was the top-performing CIBC tweet *ever* with an engagement rate 10 times the financial institution category norm. Social media engagement targets were exceeded by 201 percent (441,696 engagements) and key content delivered engagement rates 9 times higher than previous benchmarks.

One of the major lessons that we have learned from our experience with RTM was to make sure you listen first, and then answer and engage in conversation only if it is appropriate. It's not a good idea to barge in on a conversation if you've not been invited, a basic social media engagement premise.

I'm often amazed at how many organizations don't monitor what's being said about them on social media. They're missing out on a golden opportunity to connect with customers on topics that really matter to both parties. For example, a friend of mine who does a great deal of traveling to Montréal from Toronto had an experience that quickly sums up who is listening and who is not.

He was flying on Porter Airlines (a small regional carrier based at Toronto's Billy Bishop Airport), and his flight was delayed multiple times that morning, which is an unusual occurrence for Porter. He tweeted a message that suggested Porter must have been sold to Air Canada, because they were starting to have as many delays as Air Canada (ha!). Later that day, Porter responded to the tweet to apologize for the delay, but Air Canada did not respond. Air Canada obviously was not listening, so it missed an opportunity to either correct a misperception about timeliness or simply apologize and promise to do better in the future.

In order to act more like Porter and less like Air Canada, there are eight principles of Social Media 101 that you should follow; these can prepare you for the real-time challenges of customer demands.

1. #BeAware

Before doing anything, you must be aware of what's happening out there. That means listening in to social conversations to discover what your customers are talking about and whether those conversations are about your brand or something else. This requires software, hardware, trained and educated staff, and, most importantly, a process to manage the flow of information.

Once you've set that up and have been listening for a while, you can start creating posts, tweets, videos, and content that match the themes you are hearing. The end goal is to create content and responses that match the needs of the customer, while creating awareness and relevance for your brand.

A great example of this is Bank of America (BoA) and the social media "war room" that they set up during the 2009 Davos World Economic Forum in Switzerland. Experts from the bank's legal, social media, marketing, advertising, and other departments scanned 60-inch screens late into the night to see what was trending on Twitter (Figure 7.12). Their mission: To promote the bank's brand among people who are interested in economic issues by publishing

Figure 7.12   BofA takes advantage of #davoswomen trending on Twitter.

real-time content that is related to the conference. During a session on women, for example, with #davoswomen trending on Twitter, the bank's team tweeted a link to a Merrill Lynch paper about the growing economic influence of women.

The bank's use of the conference to promote its brand seems to have paid off: According to BoA, 97 percent of people who clicked on their social media content during the economic conference were engaging with the bank for the first time.

2. #BePrepared

Once you're aware of what's going on, you need to have the processes and culture in place to respond and adjust very quickly. That means having a content strategy already in place so that when the opportunity arises, you're not starting from a standing start—you're ready to respond on the fly. The 2014 Oscars provided a good example, and I don't mean Ellen DeGeneres and her mass selfie. It was NASA. Knowing that *Gravity* was up for a number of awards, NASA prepared tweets and content under #realgravity to capitalize on the exposure that the space program was getting from the movie (Figure 7.13).

Figure 7.13   Tweet from NASA during the Oscars.

3. #BeAppropriate

It goes without saying that once you put something out into social media, there's no pulling it back. Yet every day, someone or some organization is saying, "Whoops, didn't mean to say that." Brands are so eager to jump into conversations that they sometimes forget to be careful. Take a look at what Kenneth Cole posted during the Cairo protests in 2011: "Millions are in uproar in #Cairo. Rumor is they heard our new spring collection is now available online." Well, they certainly got recognition for that tweet, but none of it was good.

You can have fun, too. I like what the Belize Tourism Board did when they heard that "a trip to Belize" was used in *Breaking Bad* as a euphemism for murder. They put together a clever program offering free vacations to the Central American nation for show runner Vince Gilligan and eight members of the AMC drama's cast (Figure 7.14). The Belize Tourism Board took advantage of the

Figure 7.14   Belize Tourism Board's response to _Breaking Bad_'s use of Belize.

opportunity to show off Belize's laid-back vibe and great sense of humor, which are also Belize's great assets.

4. #BeTrue

In the world of social media, you are totally exposed. This can be extremely powerful and amazing, but if you act inconsistently with your brand's DNA, you will get caught, and you will be called out. Being true to the tone and manner of your brand DNA is critical to ensure that you act in a genuine manner. When you do, it creates a sense of authenticity and realism that makes you believable and approachable.

5. #BeCreative

Attention is a rapidly decreasing resource, and the bar to continually be noticed keeps getting higher and higher. Audiences are demanding more than the usual conversation, so if you want

Figure 7.15   Ben & Jerry's cool imagery on Instagram.

to engage them, you have to be creative. Instagram is a wonderful medium to share brand creativity because of its visual impact. Perhaps that's why Ben & Jerry's decided to invest heavily in Instagram; they deploy a combination of engaging ads and regular posts that have amassed 396,792 followers and counting (Figure 7.15).

6.   #BeBrave

In social media, you don't just compete with your competing brands; you compete with over a billion content creators—and on any day, they are faster, smarter, funnier, and more influential than you can ever be. (I know; it's sad but true.) So what do you do? Well, for one thing, being brave and being willing to stand out in a crowd can help. That's why it's important that your brand stand for something greater than the product or service that you offer. By identifying and articulating the higher values or purpose of your brand, you can establish a sustainable and memorable territory for your organization.

7. #BeResilient

Unless you have supernatural powers, at some point there's going to be a blip in your social media presence. It could be self-inflicted or come from an outside source, but the key is to take responsibility and act quickly before it gets beyond your control.

JC Penney had inadvertently sent out what looked like a drunken text, which kicked up a storm of responses from consumers, including other third-party brands joining in the discussion. JC Penney was smart and resilient by responding with a relevant tweet and product placement (Figure 7.16).

8. #BeRelevant

Staying relevant may be the most significant aspect to your social media presence. Although we all love a big, flashy media splash, often it lasts for just a short time and ends up being essentially a one-off rather than a campaign. It is much more difficult, and more rewarding, to run sustainable messaging. I have great admiration for brands that use social media in real time to deliver an engaging, consistent message about their product or services over the long term.

Walgreens has taken this principle right to the aisle by developing a social-local-mobile (SoLoMo) strategy that reaches in-store shoppers where they are most likely to buy—in the store. Here's how it works (Figure 7.17).

When customers check in at a Walgreens location, they instantly receive a coupon. This is a great example of using RTM to drive real, physical, and measurable customer behavior and establish relevance where and when it matters the most.

No one will tell you that enabling your staff and organizational processes to utilize real-time marketing is easy, but easy or not, this is the pace and environment in which your audience lives. If you want to keep up with them and be relevant for them, then that is what you need to do.

Figure 7.16   JC Penney nips a problem in the bud.

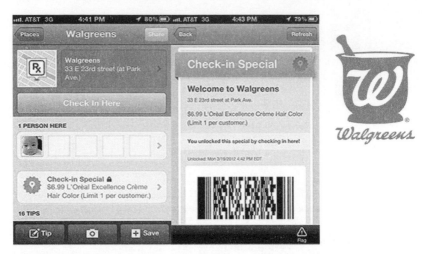

Figure 7.17   Walgreens personalizes the experience as soon as the customer walks in the door.

WHERE DO YOU START?

With lots of distribution choices and a never-ending appetite for content, businesses are now faced with trying to feed a perpetual messaging cycle with a steady flow of engaging, newsworthy content that is targeted to their various audiences. Whew. The days of the episodic one-dimensional advertising plan (e.g., this campaign runs in the first quarter) have been replaced by what I refer to as a "perpetual campaign." As organizations retool their resources to provide material for this new always-on messaging necessity, they need to get maximum value from that investment, particularly when it comes to repurposing content for multiple channels. Planning really helps, because by thinking ahead, you can build in the necessary technical and creative flexibility to adjust content for different channels. Producing good content is hard work, so you want to make sure that you're taking every possible step to create something memorable and lasting.

PLANNING

To reemphasize a previous point, it's important to take the time to plan. Publishers build a calendar to plot out their requirements and deliverables, so take a page from their book. This is a complex process, and it's easy to get distracted. Being distracted is not an option when you consider how important content is to the long-term success of your organization. Here are some steps to get you moving in the right direction.

- Understand the needs of your customers along each step of their decision journey and correlate those findings to your business goals.
- Conduct an audit of your current efforts, resources, and media presence. Look for successes and failures.
- Build an organizational structure with the commitment and capabilities to create, write, and produce content.
- Determine what your brand voice and story will be.
- Build a narrative of key moments that define and bring your brand to life for customers and employees alike.
- Create educational programs to inform employees of the program's intent and give them content development tools.
- Establish guidelines and governance to ensure consistency across the organization.
- Develop a publishing calendar to plot out content needs and how outputs will be used across owned, paid, and earned media.
- Build an archiving system to curate content for reference and reuse.
- Put one person in charge to oversee and guide your efforts, and build a multidepartment strategy to collect stories and ensure that guidelines are being followed.

While this may not be a complete list, it's enough to help you plot a new course of action or recalibrate what you currently have in place.

ALIGN DECISION MAKERS BEFORE YOU START

With your plan in hand, the next important step is to build consensus with the executive team to get them on board early, as they'll help provide input to the governance of the process. Many content priorities are issues that only the executives can solve, such as approving the right message, focus, and tone at each customer decision point, so their buy-in is critical.

Sometimes your executive team wants to suggest changes to your social media policy or the overall "voice" of your brand. By methodically working through the details with them now, you'll set benchmarks for content marketing activities that can reduce their future participation, and you'll have standards against which all initiatives can be measured. Further, by creating a single game plan, you'll give more flexibility and decision-making power to the people on the front lines, helping enable them to confidently produce content that fits with the multilevel objectives of the organization.

GETTING THE CONTENT STRATEGY RIGHT UP FRONT

Content strategy has three aims: Define the key messages; operationalize the process to publish; and deliver attention-grabbing stories on a consistent basis to targeted prospects, customers, and, in particular, your brand Advocates. None of these can be left to chance. It would be the same as not preparing for a major presentation and just hoping to wing it. If someone is willing to hear your story and is open to your ideas, why not take the time to think through and prepare thoroughly for such an opportunity?

We have found, however, that many businesses rush into developing content for social media. They simply present their product or service to potential customers, without preparing a relevant or compelling story.

Here are some questions to ask when you are building a content strategy:

- What do we want to be known for?
- What do our customers find interesting?
- Does the content fit with the brand personality?
- What were the lessons that we learned from past customers' engagements?
- Where do our customers gather their information and content (Twitter, Facebook, LinkedIn, YouTube, Digg)?
- What content assets can be imported from offline to online?
- Who are the recognized influencers that our customers trust and listen to?
- What customer action do we want the content to spur?
- How will we measure the results, and how do we course-correct as we monitor responses?
- How quickly can we respond to customer comments, feedback, and complaints?
- What are the next steps once we have engaged the customer to act?

Social media would be neither social nor relevant without exciting, interesting, informative, or humorous content—that's why a plan and checklist are so important. Used together, they deliver compelling content on a consistent basis that attracts and retains current customers and wins new ones. Isn't that what we all want?

THE SHORT STORY BEHIND STORYTELLING—CREATIVE CONSIDERATIONS

The not-so-secret secret about creating compelling and engaging content is telling stories. Why? People remember stories even when they forget everything else. There's a good reason that "numb" is part of "numbers": Just think about the last numbers-oriented

PowerPoint presentation you had to sit through. I'm not saying numbers are off limits; just wrap a story around them, and your audience will remember and thank you.

Stories add a human touch and a real-world perspective to your communication, whereas pure information, and its static nature, cannot build an emotional connection. You want content that resonates with your audience and gives you the opportunity to connect with customers on multiple levels. It could be a connection that makes them like you and what you stand for, or it could persuade them to take the next step in making a purchase—both results are important and valuable.

When you start to create your stories, forget "marketing-speak" and its associated jargon and focus on bringing your brand to life with authentic text, video, and visuals. Leave the clichés for someone else. Good writing is about clarity and simplicity, and that's a critical consideration, given the amount of information customers process every minute of every day. This is the time to tell your story through your solutions, personality, and values in order to establish a narrative that reinforces your uniqueness and how you make a difference in your customer's life.

GETTING THE STORY OUT THERE

Now the fun of actually producing material begins. Even if it's just text, say a blog or web content, you should have a writer involved who can bring the brand to life in terms of tone, manner, and values, and then channel that thinking into the product or service being offered to the customer. That's not too hard to do.

Moving up from just text is adding video, and we know that customers love video. As an added benefit, having video content often improves your SEO. However, this usually means that another level of creative and production expertise will be required. The good news is that new technologies have brought down the cost of shooting and editing dramatically. The bad news is that scripting, shooting, and editing video still require expertise—it's not easy to do well.

To produce video or any multimedia content, you have a few options. One is to build your own in-house capability that provides dedicated resources and quick turnarounds; the downside is it requires a major up-front investment. Or you can hire an external vendor to handle all of your needs, or combine both options, handling some production duties in-house and relying on an external production house for major projects.

Smart ad agencies have expanded their business model to handle their clients' basic video production in-house. It results in quicker turnarounds and less expenditure for small projects. Conversely, we've also seen video production companies expand their creative capabilities beyond shooting and editing, so they can provide a one-stop service for larger client assignments.

THE ART OF CREATING VALUABLE CONTENT

There is one more lens I'd like you to look through before jumping into the content revolution. Though there are moments of brilliance (usually in video format) and great content from some brands, the majority of online content that you see today is boring, frivolous, and just sits there in a haze of mediocrity. This is not just my opinion.

Research indicates that six of seven branded videos fail to amass even one million views. Without seeding (buying online space to get the video some exposure), research indicates that 499 of 500 fail to get even 500,000 views. The video that goes "viral" is for most part a bit of an illusion, and that's why I go back to the idea of consistency. Think about having a pure, consistent baseball swing—it enables you to hit lots of singles, some doubles, the occasional triple, and then, every once in awhile, you pop one over the fence. We think it's smarter and more productive to swing for an average hit than go for the elusive home run. Having a global viral hit is nice, but you're going to find more success by focusing on the communities and audiences that are connected to your brand, and giving them relevant and entertaining content that matches their needs.

Keep in mind that your organization's value will rise or fall based on the quality of your content. It is a new currency for brand building, and how much you invest (mentally, financially, operationally) in this valuable asset will be a key driver in how your organization succeeds or fails.

CHAPTER EIGHT

INNOVATION IN DEMANDING TIMES

———

Insight Is a Transformational
Truth of Innovation

EVERY MORNING I DRIVE TO WORK IN DOWNTOWN TORONTO from a small suburb just north of the city. During this drive, I often find myself behind a cluster of UPS trucks starting their morning runs. Over time, I have noticed that these trucks rarely drive in the left lane on their route into the city.

I always thought that this was a UPS policy and its drivers were making a thoughtful and considerate effort not to interfere with the local morning traffic flow. That certainly seemed to be a logical assumption, and I saw it as a smart policy from a very visible street-level brand.

However, I recently read an article on how UPS drivers' routes are programmed to avoid left turns and how this simple innovation increased their efficiency even when driving greater distances. The results are impressive:

- Since 2004, UPS has saved an estimated 10 million gallons of gas.
- Carbon emissions have been reduced by 100,000 metric tons—that's the equivalent of taking 5,300 cars off the road for an entire year!

Years ago, UPS realized that more traffic meant more time consumed driving, and more time consumed driving meant packages would be delivered later. This insight led UPS's innovation team to develop route-optimization plans to increase efficiency, reduce fuel consumption, and get drivers back to their centers earlier. They came up with a simple rule: Minimize—or where possible, eliminate—left-hand turns.

They found a significant cause of idling time resulted from drivers waiting to make left turns, delayed against the flow of traffic. From this insight, they then explored routes where left turns could be cut out entirely, even if it meant traveling a greater distance. The end results: More packages are being delivered in less time, gas consumption goes down, and driving in a series of right-hand loops actually reduces emissions. All of this is a result of one simple data-driven insight.

This simple insight was further refined as tracking systems improved. Sophisticated data showed how each vehicle performed during its delivery route, and UPS began to see additional opportunities where efficiencies could be improved.

The UPS case also suggests that important insights can show up in any part of an organization, and the resulting innovation can make a difference that extends across internal business units and into the community where its customers live and work.

As you know, innovation has become a very hot topic in many private and public organizations. The power of innovation and creative thinking are thought to be key ingredients in future success. This same innovative and creative mind-set is also sought in an organization's leaders, a finding supported by a recent CEO study in which 80 percent of respondents identified creativity as the most important leadership characteristic needed today.

In our dynamic and unpredictable marketplace, creative leadership needs to be more than lip service. If only it were as easy as saying, "We are an innovative, creative company." I'm sure you've seen something similar in more than a few presentation slides. The reality is that even the most forward-thinking companies are challenged to build a culture that is capable of producing a consistent flow of innovative ideas that can be converted into tangible, financially viable products or services.

This is underscored by Adobe research results, in which over 80 percent of participants said that unlocking their creative potential was the key to economic growth but only 25 percent felt they were living up to their creative potential. It seems ironic that in this time of constant change, with the realization of what's needed to succeed, so many organizations struggle to keep up.

The writing is on the wall about the importance of innovation and creativity, so why do so many companies lag behind? I'd argue that part of the problem is that many are still structured around hierarchical organizational models inherited from the Industrial Age. They rely on traditional planning processes, which in turn rely on historical trends and analytics as predictors of future events.

It's not surprising, because most senior executives love predictability; that's the way they were trained both in school and in the workplace, and their continued use of traditional business practices and marketing strategies reflect that bias. But with today's customer and marketplace moving at hyper-speed, these historically based projections may not be in sync with today's customer behaviors.

Today's marketing is more immediate and future-oriented, and a lot fuzzier to plan around, so to succeed you need an innovative and creative mind-set. In many ways, we're all being forced into becoming futurists. The old, traditional focus is hard to overcome, because senior management, especially today's senior executives, haven't been educated on how to play the innovation game. Business schools, for the most part, provide traditional business education and have only recently started to add innovation and entrepreneurial studies to their curriculum; these weren't available when most senior executives were in school. As a consequence, they were programmed to look for predictability and safety in numbers, and that mind-set still dominates many decision makers. We now understand that a marketing strategy based on past success is not the final answer; in fact, it can potentially spell danger in today's eclectic market.

Another contributor to a lack of sustainable innovation is that in the past, organizations relied on internal R&D departments as their sole source of innovative marketplace offerings. A line extension here, a new product there; it was an inside-out development process that had little customer interaction or understanding.

Then the customer took control of the story line. As customers around the globe took advantage of digital technologies and social networks, they pushed the market in directions they wanted it to go, not where business wanted it to go. As part of the transformation, the power shift saw customer-led innovations and marketplace disruptions, while organizations were left asking, "What just hit us?"

So, why did the customer take control? From my perspective, businesses either took their customers for granted or ignored their current and emerging needs. Regardless of which category they fell into, customers didn't like to be neglected. With their new power, they figured out what they needed, came up with a solution, and then used social technologies to easily share that information with their friends. In short, because businesses ignored opportunities to satisfy customer needs and neglected to establish empathetic bonds with them, customers found other solutions, and finding solutions is the core factor that drives innovation and value.

The good news is that organizations can do a much better job of harnessing innovation and using it to move business forward. That means that innovation can become a defining characteristic of your business culture. Let's look at how innovation occurs in its two basic forms.

Disruptive innovation is a form that totally reinvents the business model. Netflix is one of the better examples. They sent the corner video store to the scrap heap and are now taking on the networks and studios by producing original content.

While today it's primarily digital technologies that drive disruptive innovation, it's not always the case. AirBnB shook up the hotel industry to become a global power, with over 200,000 people per night using their service. When you consider that Hilton has about 600,000 rooms around the globe, it's quite remarkable that AirBnB started in 2007 with a couple of air mattresses in the founders' apartment.

How about Uber? The inspiration for their business was that you couldn't get a cab when you needed one. With the Uber app, your mobile phone and its GPS send out a message to the closest available driver. Once the driver is en route, you can track the driver's location on the map, and when the driver arrives, you receive a text. Factor in a fare quote and billing through your phone, and you've got a remarkably hassle-free experience, and lots of people agree. From its 2009 start in San Francisco, you can now find Uber in over 70 cities and 41 countries (and expanding)—and it has a potential valuation of more than $18 billion. Not surprisingly, Uber is getting a lot of pushback from traditional taxi operators who are seeing their business model turned upside down.

Sustaining innovation is a form that produces incremental improvements on existing products, but unlike disruptive innovation, it doesn't open new markets by identifying and satisfying a new or unknown need. It also moves at a somewhat slower pace.

This style of innovation can be seen in the example of Gillette, which continually introduces a series of new blade configurations that keep their brand "fresh" and top-of-mind. The auto industry is another good example: Every model year has something new, even when the chassis remains the same.

Both forms of innovation share a common thread around implementation: They solve problems and produce tangible outcomes. They differ from creative thinking, which is an important part of the ideation process but doesn't take it to the next step and deliver a finished product.

I mention these two forms of innovation because there is a tendency to focus on disruptive innovation at the expense of the sustaining model. However, you can't ignore the fact that sustained commitment to innovation can provide significant impact across all parts of your organization. This collective focus leads to consistent gains across the business, and that bodes well for your future.

Innovation can often come from listening to and establishing an empathetic bond with customers—at the minimum, it can let you avoid making decisions and changes that you may regret.

> *"This 'telephone' has too many shortcomings to be seriously considered as a means of communication. The device is inherently of no value to us."*
> —*Western Union internal memo, 1876*

> *"I think there is a world market for maybe five computers."*
> —*Thomas Watson, chairman of IBM, 1943*

> *"640K ought to be enough for anybody."*
> —*Bill Gates, 1981*

INSIGHTS ARE THE BEDROCK OF INNOVATIVE THINKING

Innovative thinking is about producing and acting on insights that create market-ready, customer-centric solutions, but innovation is hard to come by. First, you need the insight, a transformational truth that emerges after you've sifted through and synthesized information from customer, business, and technology sources. Then you need to tap into multiple sources to not only meet that customer need but also create a viable fit within your business model.

It's a big job, bigger than just thinking creatively. It means taking a unique insight that satisfies a customer need and implementing it within your current business model. That is the result of true innovation.

The process has multiple steps, beginning with that elusive insight. In our experience, that insight often establishes a new lens with which to view the problem and creates a jumping-off point for you to explore several different directions in solving it. Once you prioritize these directions, you look to combine the best of customer and business perspectives to generate a solution that works.

When we start a new, innovative assignment, our first task is always to obtain a complete understanding of the client's customer and business from an inside-out/outside-in vantage point; we need to build a true 360-degree view of what is ideal and what is possible (from a customer and business perspective). This may sound somewhat at odds with the free-form perception of innovative thinking, but if you don't have a framework, innovation is not going to happen.

ORGANIZING FOR INNOVATION

Most organizations are not designed to be innovation hotbeds, but many have individuals and teams in-house that can innovate. To tap those sources, senior management needs to establish the right conditions for these sources, as well as the entire organization, in order to thrive. There are a couple of considerations to keep in mind when assessing the opportunities for innovation in your organization.

The first big challenge is to convince all members of the organization that they can be creative—employees, from top to bottom, often don't think they are. We seem to forget that we were all kids once, and our imaginations were quite capable of creating just about anything.

We got older, and well . . . the Industrial Age teaching methods used for teaching us squeezed most of the creative juice out of us. It's not too late to reverse that process, however, and being creative and innovative can be fun and productive for everyone, with positive results for the bottom line.

As a leader, you need to empower your people to be creative, and you need to establish the organizational commitment, guidelines, tools, and ongoing support for them to succeed.

There are a number of attributes that characterize an innovative organization, and many can be emulated.[1]

- *Every employee understands the organizational direction of the company:* Buy-in from all employees on the direction or mission of the business is essential to ensure that innovation efforts have the right focus.
- *Every employee knows that innovation is a priority:* At the top of the list of organizational priorities is the need to embrace innovation as an integral component of the culture, not just a nice-to-have component.
- *The executive team models innovative thinking and behavior:* An innovation-focused culture absolutely starts at the top, where its importance is demonstrated and then promoted throughout the organization, often with the help of HR.

- *Open and honest communication and trusting relationships:* This is key. No one person has all of the answers; this is a system of shared learning and knowledge, where trust is an essential condition.

- *Cross-functional teams that encourage diverse viewpoints:* Siloed organizations are a death knell to an innovative culture. There needs to be diversity of skills, knowledge, and life experiences, combined with an acceptance of all groups, to create a sustainable culture of innovation.

- *Leaders who take risks and focus on delivering value:* Executives need to support risk taking so that employees are not afraid to push the envelope with well-thought-out ideas. Mistakes are accepted as learning experiences.

- *Innovative thinking balanced with the discipline to implement solutions:* Innovation without implementation is only half the equation. Innovative ideas must be balanced with the business disciplines needed to bring ideas to fruition and advance the goals of the organization.

WHAT WE'VE DONE

You'd think ad agencies would be the ideal environment for an innovation-focused culture, right? Don't they have a diverse collection of "free-thinking" employees whose daily work revolves around the development and delivery of creative solutions into the marketplace? Yet most agencies are still stuck in a hierarchal mindset, which has existed for decades and sees creativity as the sole property of the creative department. I can tell you from personal experience that the old approach doesn't work anymore; there is just too much happening.

This is especially true in digital media, with its new content needs and the challenges posed by multiple platforms, devices, usability, user experience, content creation, and technology requirements. You now need as many different, diverse people at the table as possible so that no stone is left unturned when marketing and creative strategies are built.

We operationalized the innovation process into our planning model as much as possible. Based loosely on a hub-and-spoke configuration, our framework fosters an environment of intense collaboration among our employees, client, and partner teams.

One of the biggest advantages of the "all hands on deck" approach is that the sheer diversity of our staff, with their associated expertise and experience, widens the frame of the opportunity or challenge from the beginning—it forces us to look at it from every possible angle from the very start. Sometimes this leads to opening up even bigger opportunities and can even prevent us from becoming derailed when some unforeseen problem raises its ugly head midway through.

The model is simple, flexible, and operates around the following guidelines:

- Create a flat organizational structure with subject-matter experts who bring different disciplines. For example, in our agency, we have experts in media, research, planning, analytics, creative, production, digital, and traditional aspects of marketing communications. Have everyone come to the table ready to collaborate as part of the team.

- Operate under one profit and loss statement, with one bottom line. Avoid having fragmented silos battling for revenue.

- Reinforce the idea that creativity can come from anyone and anywhere; make sure junior as well as senior team members are heard. Ideas are not the sole possession of any one individual or any one team.

- Get out of the office more. We think it's an easy way to build customer knowledge and stay current. Get out and talk to employees, talk to customers, talk to vendors, talk to the competition. Here's one example where "talk is cheap," so why not use it to gain a better understanding of the customer experience?

- Finally, don't forget to listen closely. Along with talking, we like to do lots of watching and act like ethnographers to observe how customers process the offline or online experience. It's the little things that matter.

When compared to some other organizational structures, we found the hub-and-spoke framework provides the best natural forum for collaboration and innovation among employees, clients, and customers. It enables us to drill deeply and quickly into our client's customer and business model to create innovative solutions that deliver measurable value. By removing internal revenue and departmental barriers, everyone has an interest in providing their expertise to whatever challenge comes our way.

We operate under the belief that anyone can be innovative or creative. It doesn't matter whether you're an accountant, project coordinator, or a creative chief; everyone has something to offer. What my senior management team and I strive to create is the right environment for everyone in our organization to succeed and contribute. When we hire, we target folks who aren't afraid to fail and will embrace the fact that the only safe prediction you can make is that unpredictability and change are just around the corner.

THE TORONTO SICKKIDS HOSPITAL PAIN SQUAD APP

Another great example of how an innovative solution results from a simple customer insight involves kids with cancer. For them, managing the pain caused by their disease can be a daily struggle. Sadly, this pain is often undertreated due to lack of appropriate tools to measure and understand its intensity, quality, and location. To do this properly, the medical staff needs their young patients to record exactly how they are feeling in a pain journal. The challenge is that after multiple chemotherapy and radiation treatments, many kids are too tired or discouraged to keep a detailed journal. If this data is not collected every single day, however, it's useless.

We took on the challenge, working closely with the SickKids research team to develop a first-of-its-kind iPhone application to gather the information needed for pain assessment. The initial insight came out of a day observing kids with cancer in the pediatric oncology ward. We quickly discovered a universal truth that could solve our compliance issue: "Kids want to be kids" and play. We realized that compliance could come through "gamification."

The application we designed, Pain Squad, was developed with a user interface tailored specifically for children (Figure 8.1).

Figure 8.1   Pain Squad app by The Hospital for Sick Children, Toronto.

It keeps kids motivated to fill in their pain diary twice a day by building in engagement and rewards when they do. When they complete three reports in a row, they receive a special message from headquarters, informing them that they have won a medal or are moving up in the ranks. If it feels fun, like playing, that's because it is.

The important information that the app collects not only has immediate therapeutic benefits but also helps future childhood cancer patients. By giving doctors the tools they need to understand the experience of pain from a child's perspective, Pain Squad is helping to improve the quality of life for children facing an unimaginable battle.

Since its launch, compliance rates have increased by over 90 percent. This type of compliance is unheard of in pediatric medicine. As a result of the success at SickKids Hospital, the Pain Squad is now set to roll out to four other pediatric facilities in Canada and will be made available internationally early next year.

Can you imagine how proud we are to have innovated this product? Not only that; we have also been recognized internationally for our work, winning two Cannes Gold Lions in the user experience and not-for-profit categories and beating out Windows 8, among others, to win Fast Company's "Innovation By Design" award for 2012. Pain Squad was also recognized in the WARC 100 as being one of the "World's Smartest 100 Campaigns." We were the only Canadian agency having two winning entries among the best work done around the world.

TO LEARN MORE, VISIT: SickKids Pain Squad: http://cundari.com/cases/sick-kids-pain-squad

CHAPTER NINE

THE NEW AGENCY

The New Order of Creativity

"THERE ARE THESE TWO YOUNG FISH SWIMMING ALONG, AND *they happen to meet an older fish swimming the other way, which nods at them and says 'Morning, boys. How's the water?' And the two young fish swim on for a bit, and then eventually one of them looks over at the other and says, 'What the hell is water?'"*

"This Is Water," a parable presented by David Foster Wallace in his commencement address to graduates of Kenyon College in 2005, is an eloquent description of today's marketing conundrum. To me, the two young fish highlight the challenge that we face every day making decisions in the current marketing context; our frame of reference is anchored to past experiences that are constantly being overturned or providing false direction.

CHANGE OR DIE

In January 2009, I wrote an article for *Strategy* magazine called "The New Agency Social Order" and issued a "change or die" call to all agencies, including my own. By a new social order, I'm referring to the structural changes that I see agencies needing then and today to stay viable in the years to come. It will take a new breed of marketing communications agency to create and deliver the messaging that is needed to connect with the customer in an environment where the only constant is change.

As we've discussed, agencies, like all businesses today, need a different operating philosophy and structure in order to capitalize on ideas and innovation. I'm sure that you remember when it was "the creatives" who ruled the roost. Now ideas can and should come from everywhere, and thought leadership is spread throughout the agency, depending on who has the expertise. Flattening the organization was a key driver in our own redesign, and today we see the full benefits of that in our processes, people, and, ultimately, culture.

In early 2012, we completed a three-year transition from the old integrated agency model that we had used for over 30 years to a new version that we believe is the agency of the future. You're probably thinking, "What an arrogant SOB; he thinks he has all the answers." Well, at the time, I didn't have all the answers, and frankly I still don't, but I did have the conviction, experience, and resolve to follow my beliefs about where the industry was headed. Basically, I put my money where my mouth is.

In retrospect, it was a bit of a gamble, and some things didn't go quite as planned, but we knew that if we didn't make changes, the picture would look a lot different today, and it wouldn't be a pretty one. Now that most of the work is behind us, I am happy to report that results are extremely positive, but before we get to that, let me explain the hows and whys of this transformation.

The changes we made were not arbitrary. Faced with an active marketing landscape and a new customer dynamic, we needed to ensure that changes would result in an agency that was attractive to our existing and future clients as well as ourselves.

When I started my business more than three decades ago, I was a young man. I had no preconceived ideas of what an agency was or how it should operate, let alone what services to provide.

Over the past years, there have been several big changes made to the business; I'll take you through these changes shortly. But first I want to share four governing principles that haven't changed for our agency. We identified these in those early days, and they still serve us well today.

Drive and determination to push through any challenge: I like to set goals high and then encourage the people around me to make them even higher. I find that tenacious people thrive on the energy that a challenge brings, and ultimately out of adversity comes greatness.

A sense of urgency: It's not that the big eat the small . . . it's that the fast eat the slow. We always bring a sense of urgency to everything we do, and once we're committed to a cause or idea, it needs to happen fast. The entire agency operates with the same sense of "Let's get it done."

Striving for mastery: I believe that inspiration comes from the act of striving. If I'm cooking, I want to master the dish, not just prepare it. If I'm sculpting, I want the piece to express emotions, not just duplicate the image. Mastery is ambitious and not attainable—but that's the point. I am inspired by the act of trying, and that trying and striving manifests itself in the food or the art or the work that I do.

Question everything; reframe the problem by asking "What if?": I gravitate to those who strive to discover, to the brave with the conviction to question. I find that means only the most inventive, breakthrough, and ultimately best work makes it through.

These principles have helped guide us through our first 30 years—some of our brightest times, and even through a few dark days—and they are still useful when contemplating the future of the business. Given our culture of change and belief that today's knowledge can't adequately predict what's happening tomorrow, I like to heed the advice of Alan C. Kay, founding principal of Xerox PARC:

"The best way to predict the future is to invent it."

I believe that when you're predicting the future, it's better to reframe the context in which the problem exists than try to solve the problem itself. Like the fish story, the most obvious realities are often the hardest ones to see. For example, some of the products and services that we can't live without, that have totally reshaped our marketplace, are things we didn't even know we needed.

Let's take the smartphone and tablet. At first, many of us thought, "What am I going to do with that?" and now, thousands of applications later, they have usurped the landline and computer in their daily usage.

As an entrepreneur and business owner, I'm always trying to be quick to identify and adapt to change, and from its onset the agency has taken some pretty interesting and brave restructuring efforts to keep up.

In the early 1980s, we were one of the first to commit to desktop publishing, "WYSIWYG" ("what you see is what you get"—catchy, yes?) as it was referred to at the time. We built software to enhance digital typesetting on a desktop system—a first-of-its-kind editing software that did type kerning and font tracking. This led to another innovation, and another, until we had one of the first completely digital systems for page makeup and artwork production by the end of the 1980s.

Then, with the introduction of digital photography, we set up the first completely digital photography studio with an end-to-end digital photo process. Those early days were mostly beta versions and very clumsy to use—shooting color then meant shooting multiple photos with different color filters put together by computer and converted to a usable format. However, we were the *only* photography studio in Canada that could digitally shoot a full automobile at the time. We were first because we questioned the norms, reframed the problem, and invented the technology needed to make it happen.

That spirit of discovery and innovation continues to this day; we are still developing new ideas and building them in-house on a regular basis. Our shared passion for innovation manifests itself in Cundari Labs, an expanding R&D arm of the agency that we fund to develop proprietary software for the agency and its clients. We also reach outward to acquire organizations to fill gaps or help us move forward into new service areas, especially when it comes to technology.

Through it all, our governing principles and the commitment to customer centricity have helped us grow while keeping our focus. There are a few more traits we share that have guided us to this point:

First: Because we have stayed independent, we can follow our instincts into the future and actively pursue "what's next?" wherever it may lead us.

Second: Our culture attracts really special, talented people who share in the belief of the power of customer centricity and bring their knowledge, skills, and entrepreneurial spirit to the agency. And because the agency delivers on these qualities, our people thrive.

Last, but not least: We continue to navigate the challenging seas of the new marketing world with imagination, good fellowship, and joy in a job well done.

Before we changed anything at all in the agency, we sat down with clients to build a deeper understanding of the challenges that they faced and what they required from us, their agency, in this new environment.

We then implemented a skill-set assessment of the staff with the goal of identifying employees who were multidisciplined, collaborative, innovative and, more importantly, had the desire to acquire new skills. I knew that those characteristics would be pivotal in the successful implementation of the new agency model.

We knew change would not happen overnight and, instead, prepared for a process that would be evolutionary and replicable, one where our assumptions would be tested and validated in real time.

FROM THE CLIENT POINT OF VIEW

One of the first lessons from our client research helped us understand the decision-making process when selecting an agency partner. One option, to work with a group of specialized agencies (digital, traditional, promotional, etc.), posed a few problems. From a management perspective, it can create a lot of work—briefing different agencies, administration issues such as monitoring fees, the duplication of services, multiple billing formats/processes, and the like. Then there is the issue of how well these various groups will work together (especially if they see each other as competitors, not collaborators), and for a client, that might translate into missed opportunities. In addition, there's a risk that the agency could lose focus, being less about doing good work and more about vying for a bigger piece of the pie. At the end of the day, the decision comes down to a basic question: "Is the sum of the parts worth it?"

At the opposite end is the option of a big agency, with all operating units under one banner, that can "do it all." Unfortunately, unless you're a big-spending major client, you quickly learn that the talent pool isn't all that deep. Further, often these operating units are separate cost centers, so there still will be competition for budgets, negating the benefit of "one agency."

Clients are often left with two distinct choices: Assemble a group of single-discipline agencies into a framework of integrated services or look to a single-supplier solution with all of the elements separate but in-house. They both have pluses and minuses, and I look at it this way: If you assemble a bicycle from the best available parts on the market, it will not guarantee the fastest or best ride ever assembled. The sum of all parts must provide optimal efficiencies while enhancing the performance of other parts.

Knowing this, we strove to create a third option for clients in our new agency model and believe we have. But first here are some words of caution on implementing change to become the agency of the future: "The devil is in the details."

MOVING FORWARD THE CUNDARI WAY

Our thinking was that there had to be a better way, and our guiding light during the change process was Occam's Razor, with a healthy dose of the KISS factor thrown in ("Keep it simple, stupid").

We started by using the data from our research study of over 200 CMO/marketing executives; we wanted to understand trends, structures, processes, and effectiveness, and develop actionable insights. Then we combined firsthand experience and knowledge with these studies, and narrowed the focus down to the five key areas that we believed would transform us into the agency of the future. Here are the five key areas that we came up with:

1. *We want employees with intelligence:* Quite simply, we need to make sure that the agency has the best talent available and build a culture that encourages great collaborative and innovative thinking based on deep customer understanding and empathy for customer-centric solutions in both traditional and nontraditional environments.

2. *Great work "has to work" to be great:* I know it seems obvious, but we must build programs that work. Clients want solutions that create value—not awards, reputations, or promises. They're looking for business and customer insights that generate measurable and profitable outcomes.

3. *Digital expertise is nonnegotiable:* Employees must be fluent in both digital and traditional marketing. Taking it a step further, we will invest r&d money to establish digital thought leadership and competitive advantages for our clients and ourselves. This not only attracts clients but also entices talent to join our agency rather than another agency.

4. *New partnership model:* Clients like the idea that agencies are willing to put some "skin in the game"—be more accountable and share risk. When possible, we build in a "performance pay" component to demonstrate our commitment to our client's success.

5. *Insight-rich understanding:* Clients need high-level thinking partners at the table. To ensure we deliver, we bring together the best strategic and planning talent available across a number of disciplines: those who aspire to know our clients' business better than they do. We can't rely on third-party or public information, because everyone has it. Creating this level of insight intensity means adding specialized people and processes who seek out unique insights across all aspects of the brand and its customers.

WITH THESE LESSONS, WE MADE THE FOLLOWING CHANGES

We eliminated silos once and for all: Silos are good for grain, not for agencies. We saw the advantage of a one-team rather than a teams approach, so we had to get rid of the silos and flatten the hierarchy. Bingo! We immediately saw a number of benefits. The new model enhanced our ability to develop solutions faster and get them to market faster, which resulted in a bigger return for our clients.

With a single P&L and one rate for all agency services, it was easier on our clients to manage (albeit harder for us). Yes, it was necessary to retool the revenue model from the ground up, but the result was even better staff retention due to an energetic, collaborative, and egoless culture that encouraged contributions from all employees.

Revitalized recruiting and retraining of staff: The needs of our business model directly influence our hiring practices. We now look for employees with an integrated, curious mind-set who can adapt quickly and acquire new skills. We added people with digital skills in user experience, interactive design, information architecture, content development, and programming. We put together ongoing training programs, and with the removal of silos, this allowed us to mix and match employees from different disciplines on projects—this has been the best benefit of all. Our efforts have paid off by getting and cultivating some exceptional talent. The one-team framework has added an additional catalyst for learning, cemented our collaborative culture, and improved our retention numbers. I'd say it was worth all the effort.

Research is not an afterthought: To develop deep insights into customer behavior, you can't always wait for the client to fund research projects. To that end, we have invested in skilled researchers and facilitators, built our own internal research facility, and developed our own proprietary research to help build our clients' brands.

Measure, measure, measure: Data, whether big or small, is on everyone's must-have list today. However, the ability to create meaningful analytics remains the biggest challenge. A great strategy without measurement is not a strategy, so we built out social media listening platforms, marketing metrics dashboards, and proprietary applications to capture customer feedback and transactional data and produce actionable analytics. The biggest outcome is that it enables our client and agency team to adapt to changing market conditions in real time.

"We've redesigned our processes around where decisions are made (not based on organizational structure), and retooled our processes for speed."

ANALYTICS THAT GENERATE ROI

All great insights have their root in the organization's ability to plan, gather, and decode data, and transform those findings into actionable information, which can be used in real time to further the goals of the brand. In the past, research analytics happened less frequently, such as every quarter. As a result, the findings were lagging indicators of what was happening in the market-place. In today's fast-paced marketing environment, that's too late.

To stay connected to the customer, you need the ability to generate, collect, and analyze data and use those insights to build and strengthen the brand–customer relationship in real time. A good analytical starting point is to base data collection around an explicit hypothesis about the current and unmet needs of your customers, which can lead you to create value for customers throughout the purchase journey.

Next, make sure your data is centralized. To often we are told that the data is centralized, but in fact, it resides in different business groups within the company, effectively blocking the organization's ability to harmonize data and make it actionable.

Lastly, and probably more important, management must champion these programs so that insights translate into effective action.

OUR NEW "TEAM-CENTRIC" MODEL

One of the key outcomes from our efforts to retool the agency is our "team-centric" approach to strategic planning and program development. We wanted to emphasize our core competencies, such as speed, agility, and meaningful customer experiences, to align ourselves with today's customer.

Discipline-agnostic account teams are at the center of our model; they orchestrate the agency's resources and represent the client and customer Advocate. In that role, the account team leader pulls in subject-matter experts from many areas, such as strategic planning, project management, creative development, digital media, interactive design, data and analytics, customer research, or media planning. They become players in our team-centric model, and their importance to the project is determined right from the start—they contribute accordingly. That works to avoid the problem of adding new members or disciplines halfway through only to discover that a strategy or tactic is not feasible or prohibitively expensive.

With a team-centric model, the strategic and creative development processes overlap and work as one cohesive unit. Strategy is developed and agreed to right up front, so creative flows seamlessly from it; the creative teams and the strategic planner work together throughout the entire process. This has been an enormous benefit to clients and the agency alike. The net result are creative strategy and strategic creativity.

In summary, we redesigned our business model around a deep understanding of customer decision points (moments of truth) where customer interactions with the brand can take place. Then we supported this with a diverse staff who possess the right skill sets to create highly effective and faster in-market solutions that make a tangible difference in today's competitive marketplace.

An unexpected side benefit of this redesign is a culture that attracts the most talented and innovative people in the industry, and gives them an environment in which they thrive. A "soft" testament to our culture is the significant number of people who over the past several years left for what they believed were greener pastures, only to return within a very short time, stating they "missed us." We all share in the belief that by staying focused on the customer, striving to create in a collaborative workspace, working as a "team," not "teams," and rewarding "what if?" brave thinking that pushes the limits of ideas and creativity makes us one of the best in the business.

Of this, I am both humbled and very proud.

CONCLUDING THOUGHTS

A New Order of Business

KEEP IT REAL

We've looked at how customer centricity and understanding the new customer purchase journey can be the key to success for organizations of any size. And yet achieving this goal can be difficult, elusive at best. While we recognize changes unfolding in front of us, our organizations seem totally unprepared to let go of old methods, cultures, and thinking that are significantly out of step with evolving customer expectations.

I honestly think that as technology gets smarter, we humans are getting dumber when it counts. We seem to be living in the moment. Instead of living through experiences, we fill our lives with stuff—a great deal of it digital. Here lies the real challenge for businesses and individuals: How do you build a real relationship, which takes time to develop, if you only get a moment? How do you create relationships with people who are increasingly isolated or living in a self-induced digital bubble when these relationships are online and built around tweets?

I'm betting the answer lies in communications that revolve around simplicity, empathy, and intimacy, and this approach does not just apply to customers; it applies to everyone in your organization. There is no better example than the shoemaker and how he built his business around quality products, superior experience, and intimate customer knowledge. I leave you with the three thoughts that are constants when building a relationship with your customers: Keep it simple, keep it human, and keep your customer.

KEEP IT SIMPLE

The most difficult trick to pull off is to keep what we do simple. We seem to want to build communication strategies that make us sound and look smarter, and reflect positively on us, rather than provide a clear message with underlying value that simplifies our customer's life. It's easy to get caught up in technology's shiny objects, but at the end of the day, it's not the shiny objects that build business; it's relationships. Customers who engage with us and believe in what we stand for create long-term loyalty and profitability.

KEEP IT HUMAN

With the overwhelming influx of new technology and the digitization of nearly every aspect of our lives, I believe we are dehumanizing our relationships and creating superficial connections with no real, deep meaning. I sense that we are losing the ability to empathize with one another and, as a consequence, those deep emotional connections that are the foundation of great communicators. As communicators, we need to listen and be ready to engage whenever and wherever our customer is willing to connect. We must demonstrate empathy in our messaging, processes, and systems to build emotional bonds. When we do, customers will interact with our brands in ways that go beyond our highest expectations.

KEEP YOUR CUSTOMER

In real estate, it's "location, location, location." For us, like the shoemaker, it's all about knowing the customer and knowing him or her better than anyone else. This will be our and your key to success.

Business environments will change and technology will evolve, but one thing will remain constant, and that is the need for close personal relationships and acceptance. Knowing your customers and how you contribute and provide value to them will drive the success of your organization now and in the future.

In closing, this is a new age for all organizations. Big or small, private or public, product- or service-based, it doesn't really matter; the new customer is making and changing the rules. At the center of all this new age stands marketing, with the people, tools, insights, and desire to play a leadership role in creating the customer connections and relationships that enable our organizations to thrive.

I wish you much luck in that endeavor.

NOTES

CHAPTER 1: THE AGE OF THE CUSTOMER

1. www.softschools.com/timelines/industrial_revolution_timeline/40.

2. Robert E. Lucas Jr., *Lectures on Economic Growth* (Cambridge: Harvard University Press, 2004), 109–10.

3. Bournemouth University, "Defining Marketing," accessed January 20, 2015, http://media3.bournemouth.ac.uk/marketing/02defining/01history.html.

4. Louis Boone and David Kurtz, *Contemporary Marketing*, 16th ed. (Mason, OH: South-Western, Cengage Learning, 2014), 9.

5. James E. Stoddard, "Marketing: Historical Perspectives," in *Encyclopedia of Business and Finance*, 2nd ed., ed. Burton S. Kaliski (Detroit, MI: Macmillan Reference USA, 2007), 16, http://www.encyclopedia.com/doc/1G2–1552100211.html.

6. T. S. Ashton and Pat Hudson, *The Industrial Revolution, 1760–1830 (OPUS)* (Oxford, England: Oxford University Press, 1998); Charles More, *Understanding the Industrial Revolution* (Oxon, England: Routledge, 2000).

CHAPTER 2: CARPE DIEM

1. Accessed from http://www.retailcustomerexperience.com/articles/survey-twice-as-many-people-tell-others-about-bad-service-than-good/.

2. IBM Corporation, *From Stretched to Strengthened: Insights from the Global Chief Marketing Officer Study* (Armonk, New York: IBM Corporation, 2011), 15, http://public.dhe.ibm.com/common/ssi/ecm/gb/en/gbe03419usen/GBE03419USEN.pdf.

3. ICA and TerraNova Market Strategies, "A Wise Head on an Energetic Body: The Needs of Marketers Today and How Communications Agencies Can Best Bring Value," 2013, 5–7.

CHAPTER 3: CUSTOMER RELATIONSHIPS HAVE CHANGED

1. "United Breaks Guitars," YouTube video, 4:37, posted July 6, 2009 by "Sons of Maxwell," http://youtu.be/5YGc4zOqozo.

2. Bob Garfield and Doug Levy, *Can't Buy Me Like: How Authentic Customer Connections Drive Superior Results* (New York: Penguin Group, 2013), 27–30.

3. http://trendandtonic.thefuturescompany.com/june-2014-infographic-corporate-social-responsibility.

4. Tracey Stokes and David Cooperstein, "How Branded Content Will Unlock The Key to Consumer Trust," Forrester Research, 2013, 5, https://www.forrester.com/How+Branded+Content+Will+Unlock+The+Key+To+Consumer+Trust/-/E-PRE4784.

5. http:// axelletess.tumblr.com/day/2013/06/19; Louise Story, "Anywhere the Eye Can See, It's Likely to See an Ad," *New York Times*, January 15, 2007, http://www.nytimes.com/2007/01/15/business/media/15everywhere.html; Jay Walker-Smith, Yankelovich Consumer Research.

6. Ewan Duncan, Eric Hazan, and Kevin Roche, *iConsumer: Digital Consumer Customers Altering the Value Chain*, McKinsey & Company, April 2013, 3–5, http://www.mckinsey.com/insights/telecommunications/developing_a_fine-grained_look_at_how_digital_consumers_behave.

7. Ibid.

CHAPTER 4: FROM FUNNEL TO THE JOURNEY

1. David Court, Dave Elzenga, Susan Mulder, and Ole Jørgen Vetvik, "The Consumer Decision Journey," McKinsey & Company, June 2009, 1–4, http://www.mckinsey.com/insights/marketing_sales/the_consumer_decision_journey.

2. Ibid.

3. Brian Solis, *What's the Future of Business? Changing the Way Businesses Create Experiences.* (Hoboken, NJ: John Wiley & Sons, 2013), 62.

4. Jim Licenski, *Winning the Zero Moment of Truth*, Google eBook, http://books.google.com/books/about/Winning_the_Zero_Moment_of_Truth.html?id=JU4J58bum24C, 9.

5. Google/Shopper Sciences, "The Zero Moment of Truth Macro Study," April 2011, https://www.thinkwithgoogle.com/research-studies/the-zero-moment-of-truth-macro-study.html.

6. A. G. Afley, the CEO of P&G—First Moment of Truth (FMOT) and Second Moment of Truth (SMOT).

7. Ewan Duncan, Eric Hazan, and Kevin Roche, "Digital Disruption: Evolving Usage and the New Value Chain," McKinsey & Company, 2013, 2, http://mckinseyonmarketingandsales.com/digital-disruption-evolving-usage-and-the-new-value-chain.

CHAPTER 5: BRANDS WILL NEVER BE THE SAME

1. Jim Stengel, *Grow: How Ideals Power Growth and Profit at the World's Greatest Companies* (New York: Crown Business, 2011), 10.

2. Ibid., 38.

3. Simon Sinek, Start with *Why: How Great Leaders Inspire Everyone to Take Action* (New York: Penguin Group, 2009), 41.

4. Joey Reiman, *The Story of Purpose: The Path to Creating a Brighter Brand, a Greater Company, and a Lasting Legacy* (Hoboken, NJ: John Wiley & Sons, 2012), 14.

5. IBM Corporation, From Stretched to Strengthened, 35.

6. Paul Hagen, "How to Build a Customer-Centric Culture," Paul Hagen's Blog, Forrester Research, February 14, 2011, http://blogs.forrester.com/paul_hagen/11–02–14-how_to_build_a_customer_centric_culture.

CHAPTER 6: CUSTOMER EXPERIENCE STRATEGY

1. IBM Corporation, "IBM Project Northstar—IBM's Vision and Strategy for Exceptional Web Experiences" (white paper), September 2010, 2.

2. Bodine, "Top 10 Ways to Improve Digital Experiences," Kerry Bodine's Blog, Forrester Research, September 7, 2012, http://blogs.forrester .com/kerry_bodine/12–09–07-top_10_ways_to_improve_your_digital_ customer_experience.

3. IBM Institute for Business Value, "The Customer-Activated Enterprise: Insights from the Global C-suite Study," IBM Corporation, 2013, 7, http://public.dhe.ibm.com/common/ssi/ecm/gb/en/gbe03572usen/ GBE03572USEN.PDF.

4. Avinash Kaushik, *Web Analytics 2.0: The Art of Online Accountability & Science of Customer Centricity* (Indianapolis, IN: John Wiley & Sons, 2010).

5. R. Rogowski, "How to Build and Implementation Road Map for Your Digital Experience Strategy." Forrester Research, 2011.

CHAPTER 7: BUILDING RELATIONSHIPS WITH THE ADVOCATE/ SHARECASTER

1. Forrester's 2013 North American Technographics Survey.

2. New York Times Customer Insight Group, "The Psychology of Sharing: Why Do People Share Online?," 2013, 15–18, http://nytmarketing. whsites.net/mediakit/pos.

3. Ahava Leibtag, "Creating Valuable Content: An Essential Checklist," Content Marketing Institute, April 5, 2011, http:// contentmarketinginstitute.com/2011/04/valuable-content-checklist.

CHAPTER 8: INNOVATION IN DEMANDING TIMES

1. David S. Weiss and Claude P. Legrand, *Innovative Intelligence: The Art and Practice of Leading Sustainable Innovations in Your Organization* (Mississauga, Ontario: John Wiley & Sons, 2011), 129–31.

INDEX